Creative Christmas
Coloring

by Christina Rose

Classic Christmas themes and patterns for a peaceful and relaxing holiday season

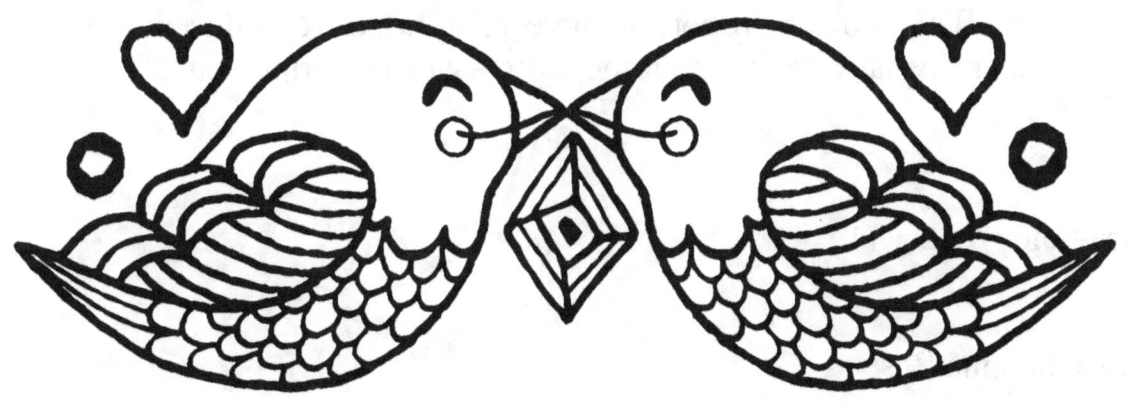

Creative Christmas Coloring
Classic Christmas themes and patterns for a peaceful
and relaxing holiday season

First published in the United States in 2015 by
Bell & Mackenzie Publishing Limited

ISBN: 978-1-910771-46-4

Created by Christina Rose
Contributors: Laura Vann

www.bellmackenzie.com

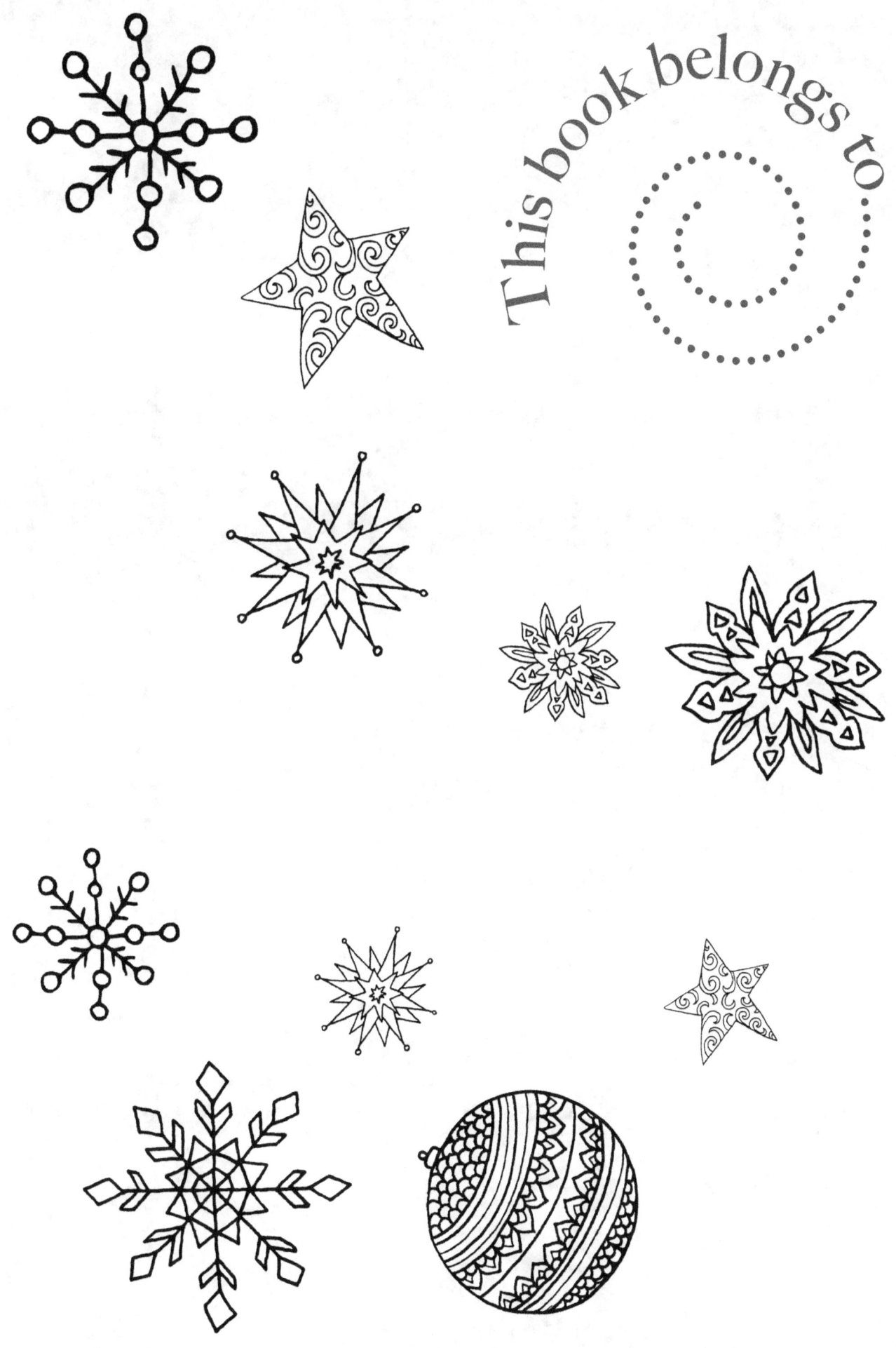

This book belongs to

Christmas waves a magic wand over this world, and behold, everything is softer and more beautiful.

Norman Vincent Peale

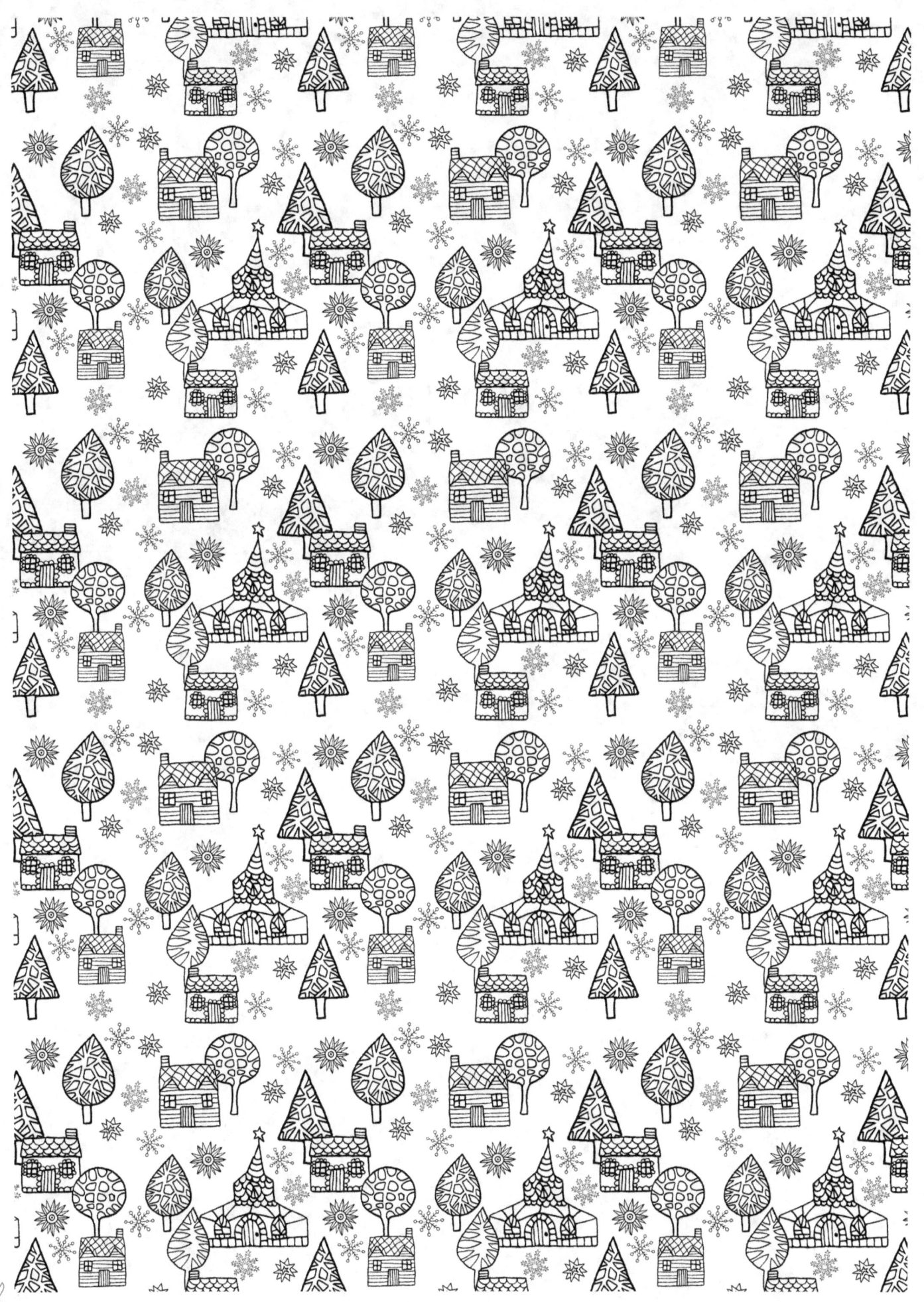

He who has not Christmas in his heart will never find it under a tree.

Roy L. Smith

Christmas is the gentlest, loveliest festival of the revolving year — and yet, for all that, when it speaks, its voice has strong authority.

W.J. Cameron

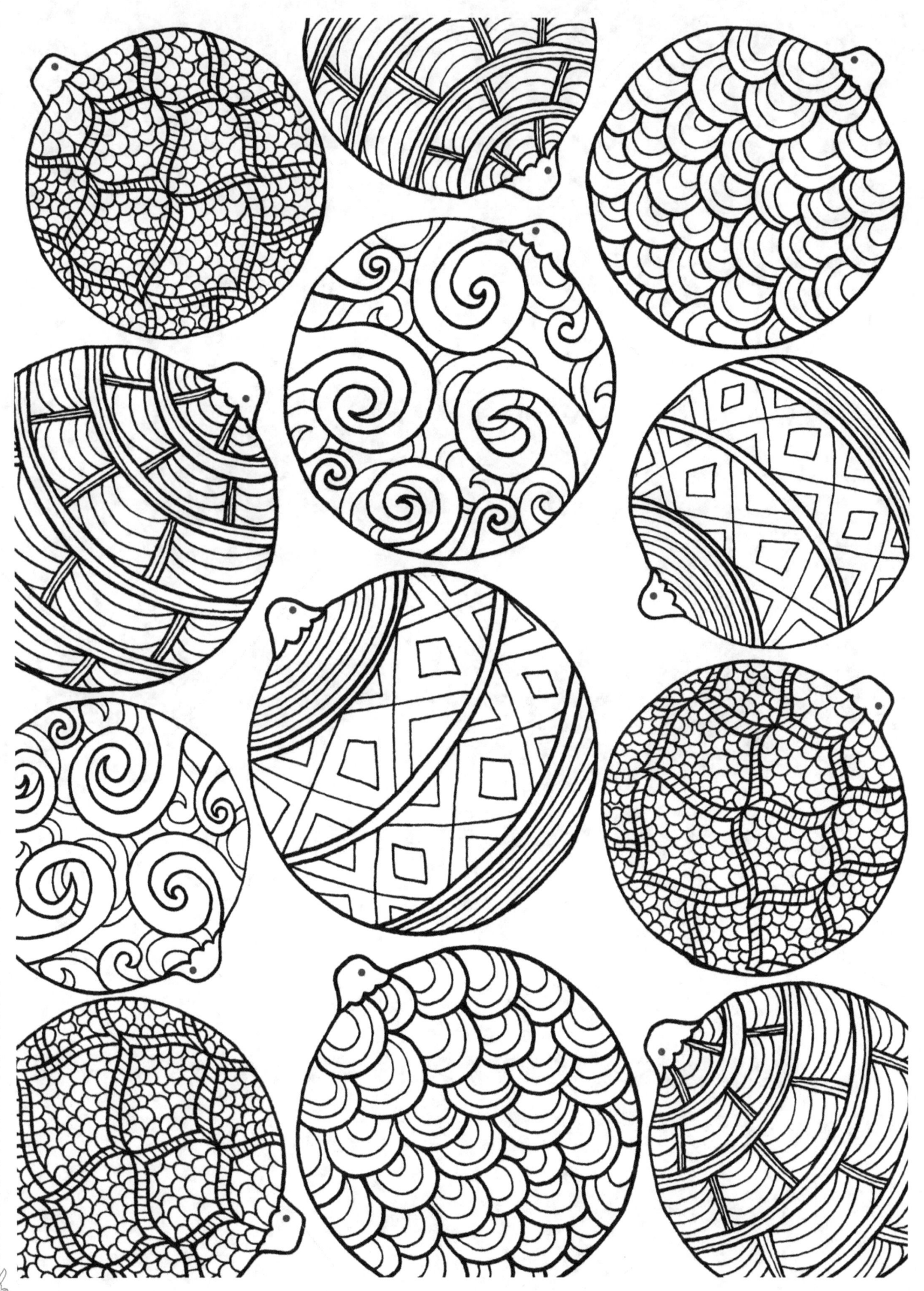

The best of all gifts around any Christmas tree: the presence of a happy family all wrapped up in each other.

Burton Hillis

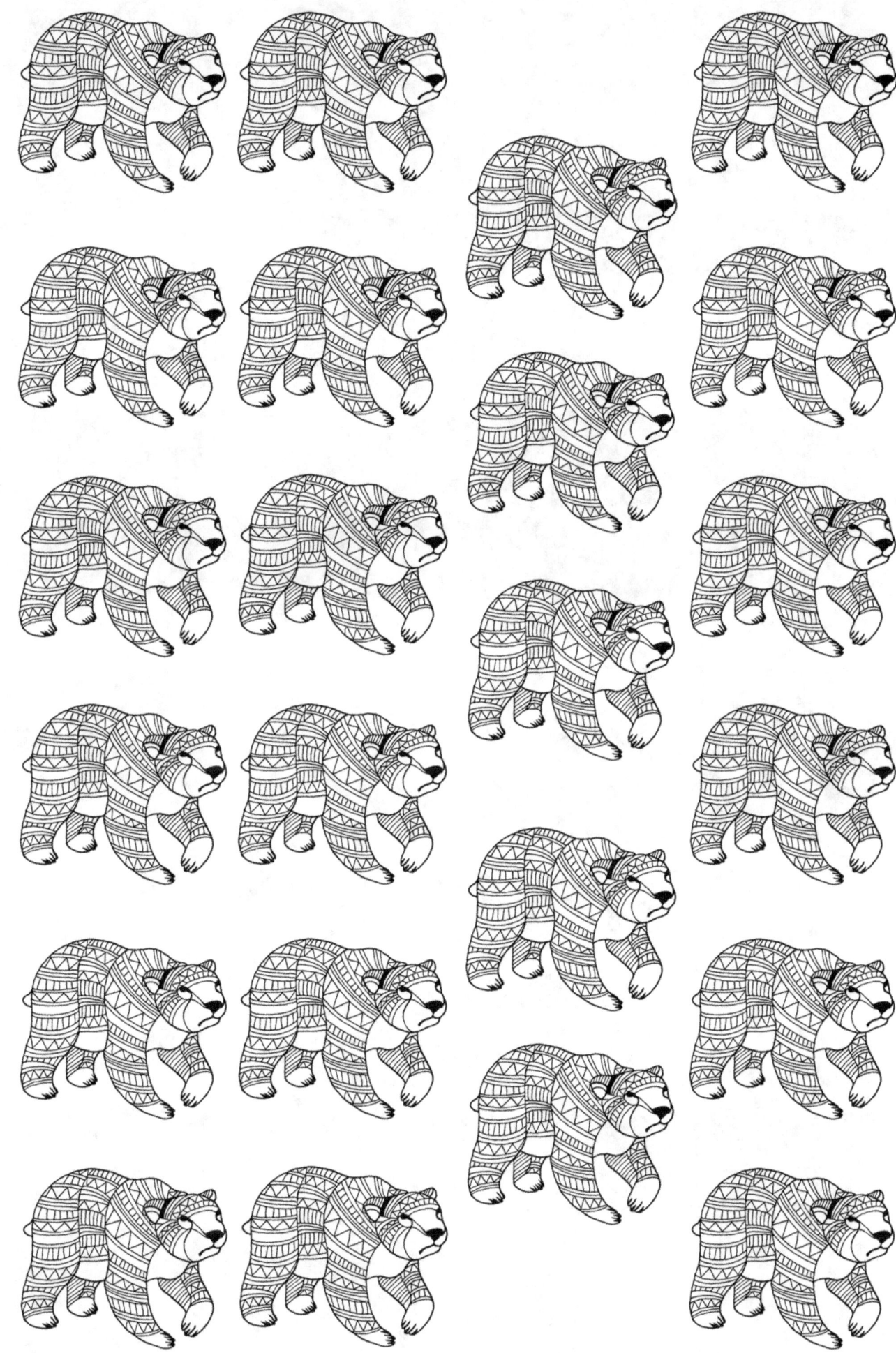

Happy, happy Christmas, that can win us back to the delusions of our childish days; that can recall to the old man the pleasures of his youth; that can transport the sailor and the traveller, thousands of miles away, back to his own fire-side and his quiet home!

Charles Dickens

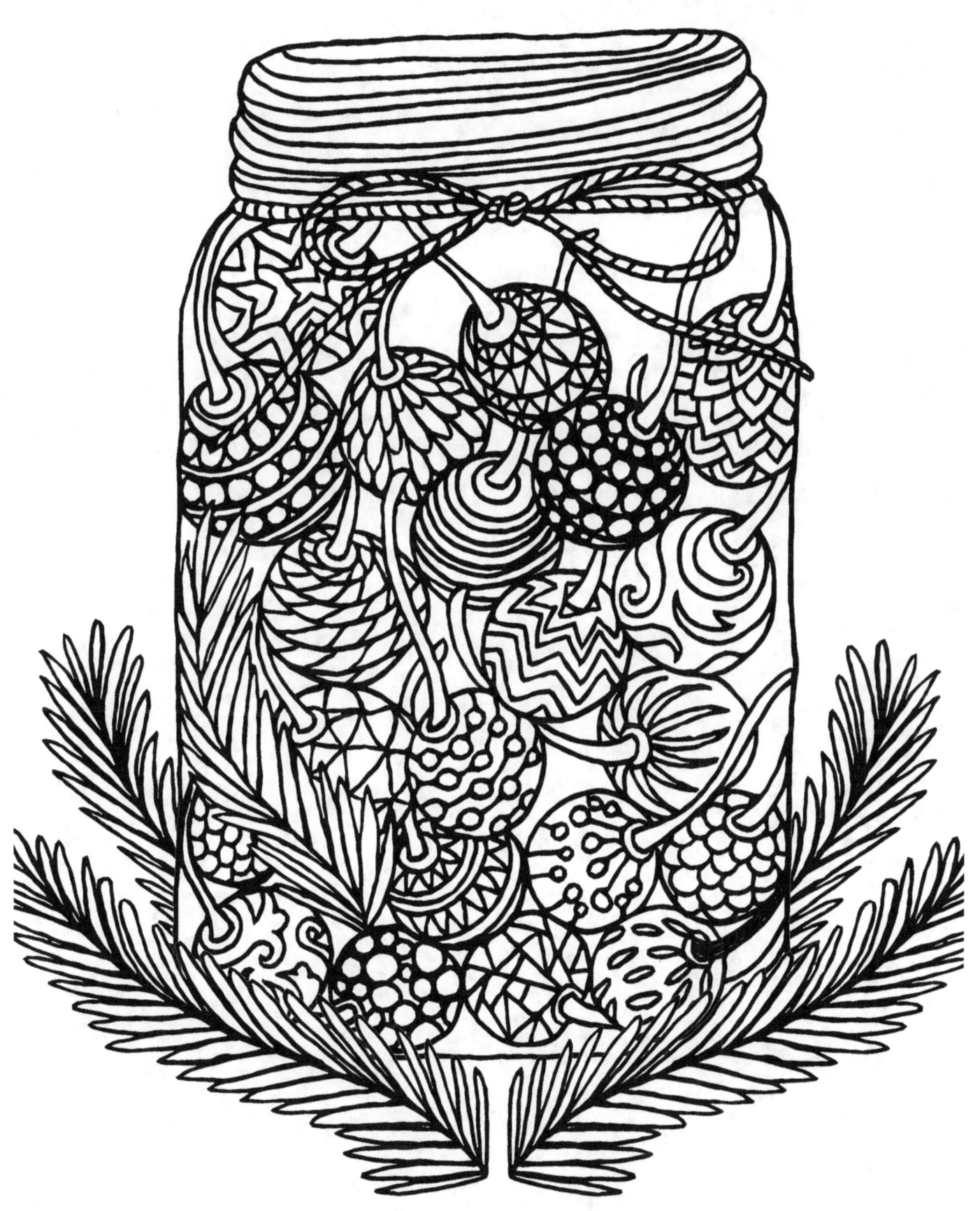

Christmas is a necessity. There has to be at least one day of the year to remind us that we're here for something else besides ourselves.

Eric Sevareid

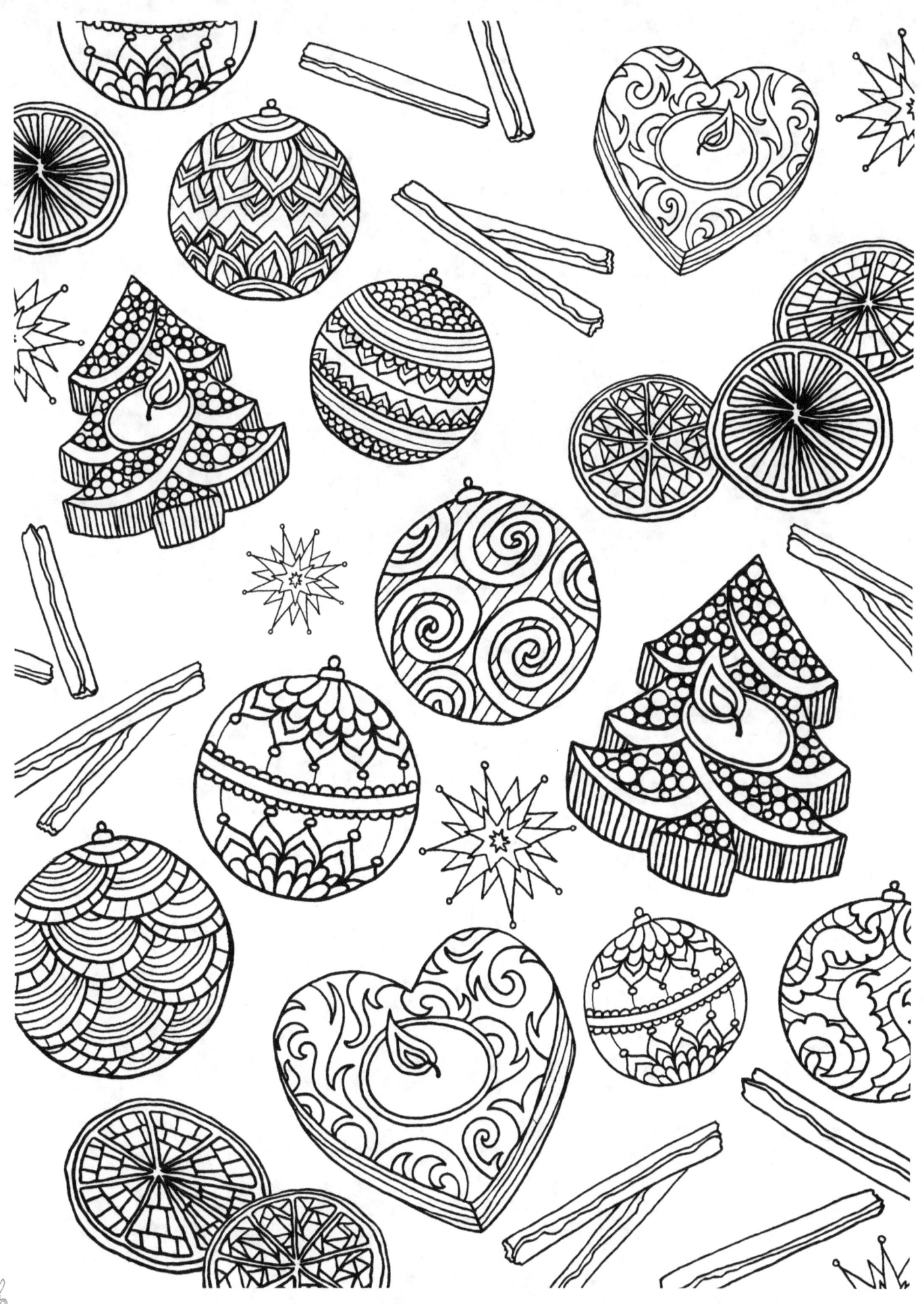

Our hearts grow tender with childhood memories and love of kindred, and we are better throughout the year for having, in spirit, become a child again at Christmas-time.

Laura Ingalls Wilder

A lovely thing about Christmas is that it's compulsory, like a thunderstorm, and we all go through it together.

Garrison Keillor

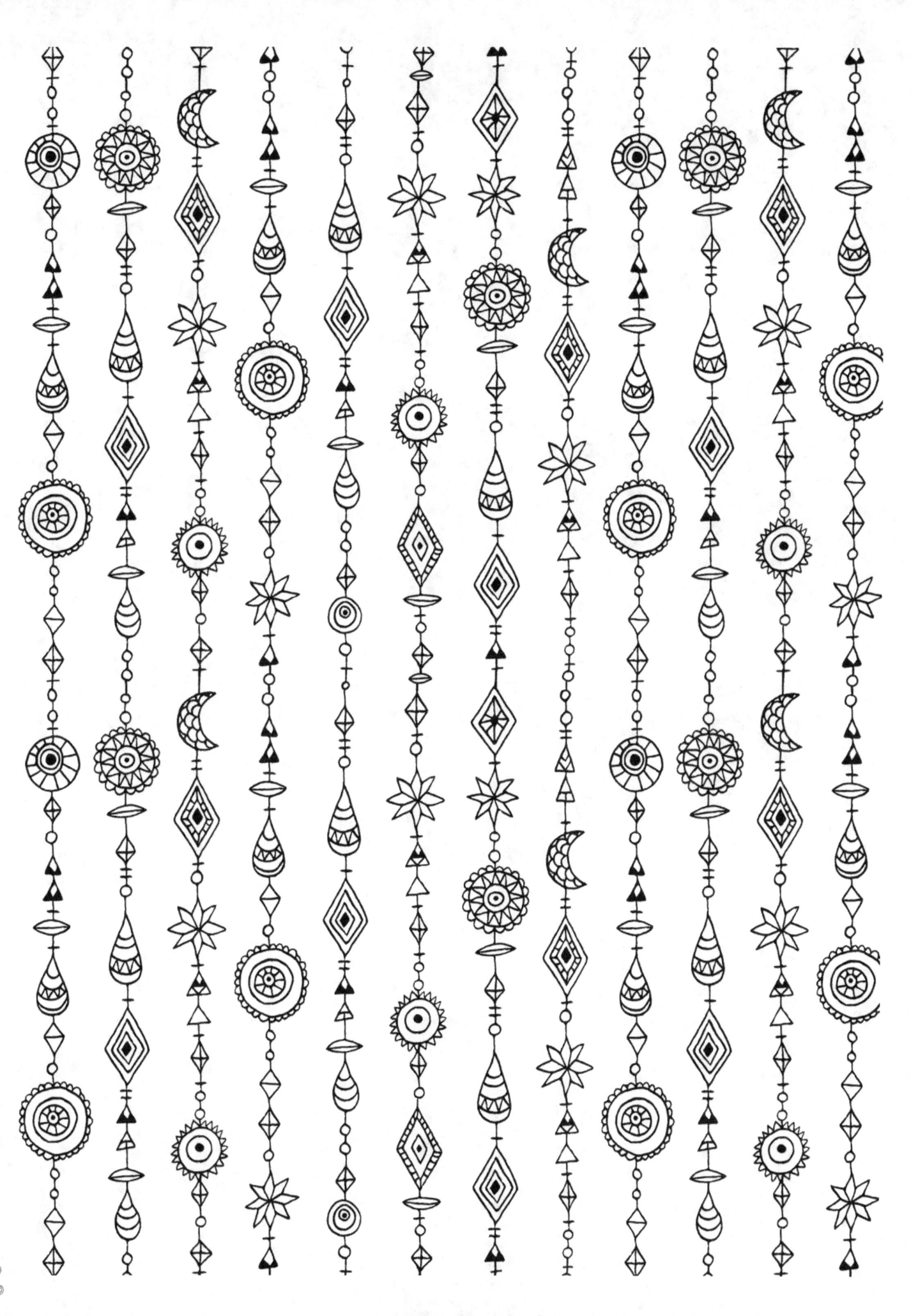

Mankind is a great, an immense family.... This is proved by what we feel in our hearts at Christmas.

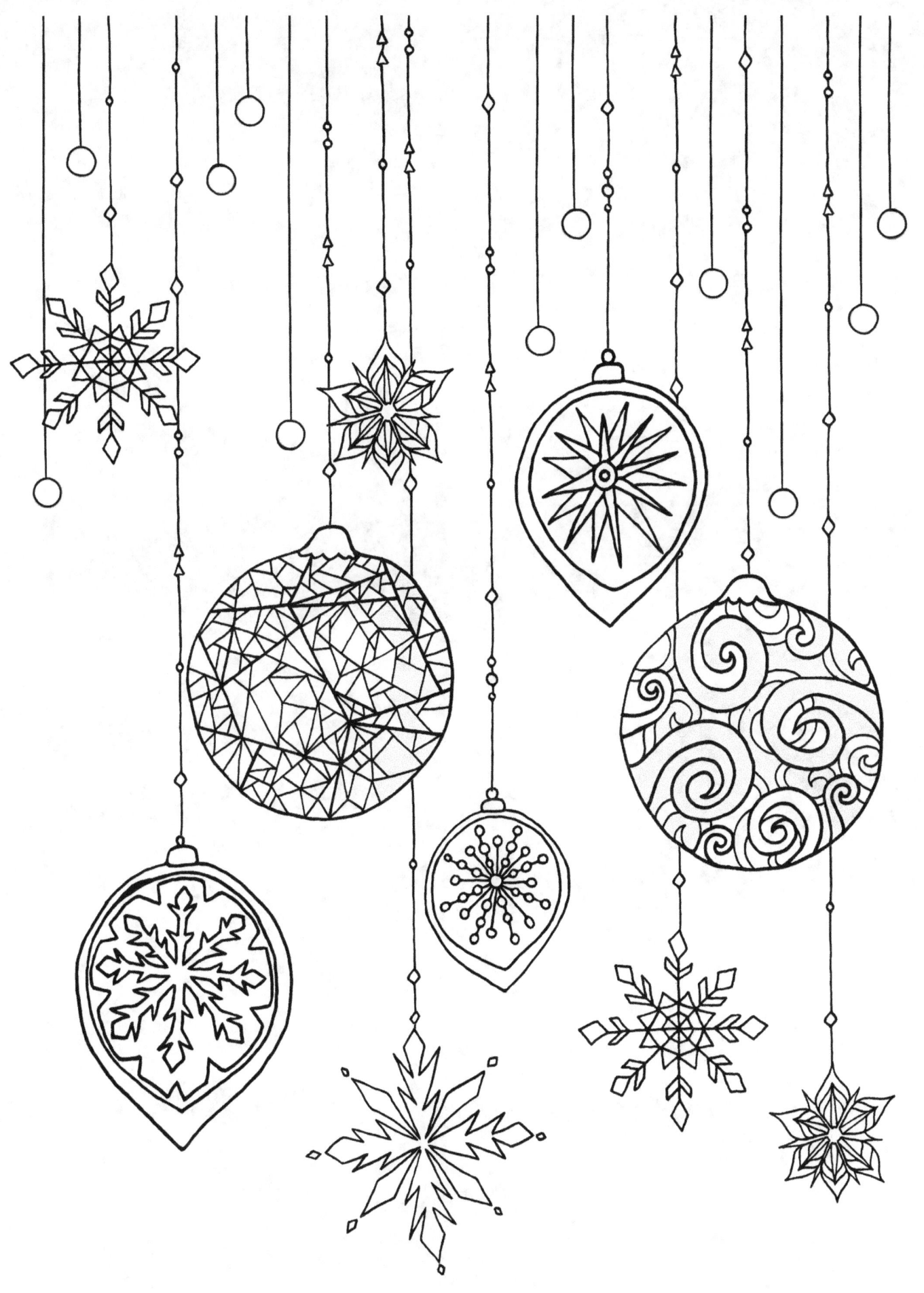

Christmas is forever, not for just one day. For loving, sharing, giving, are not to put away like bells and lights and tinsel, in some box upon a shelf. The good you do for others is good you do yourself.

Norman Wesley Brooks

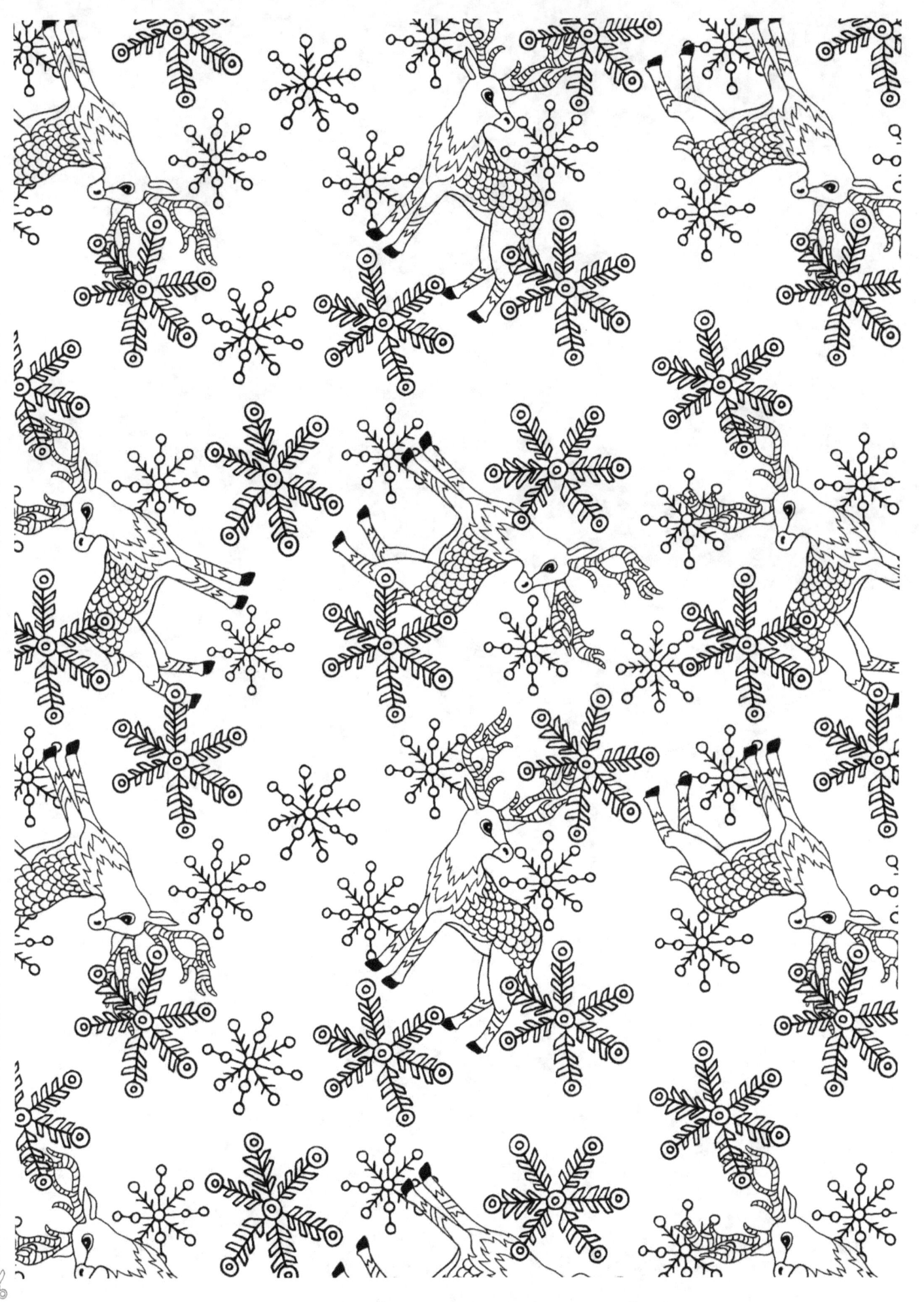

And, so, Christmas comes to bless us! Comes to teach us how to find the joy of giving happiness and the joy of being kind.

Gertrude Tooley Buckingham

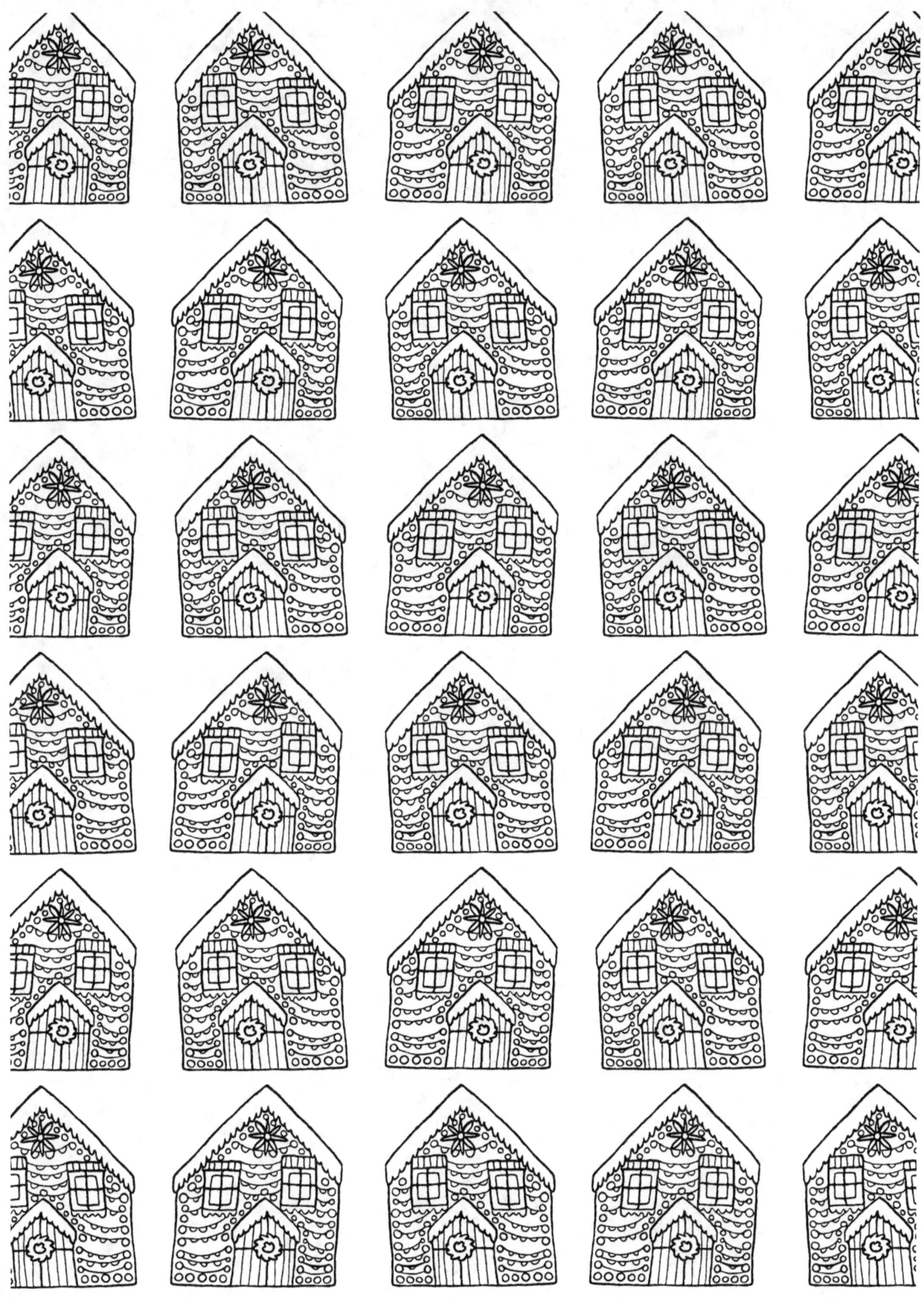

Christmas is for children. But it is for grown-ups too. Even if it is a headache, a chore, and nightmare, it is a period of necessary defrosting of chill and hide-bound hearts.

Lenora Mattingly Weber

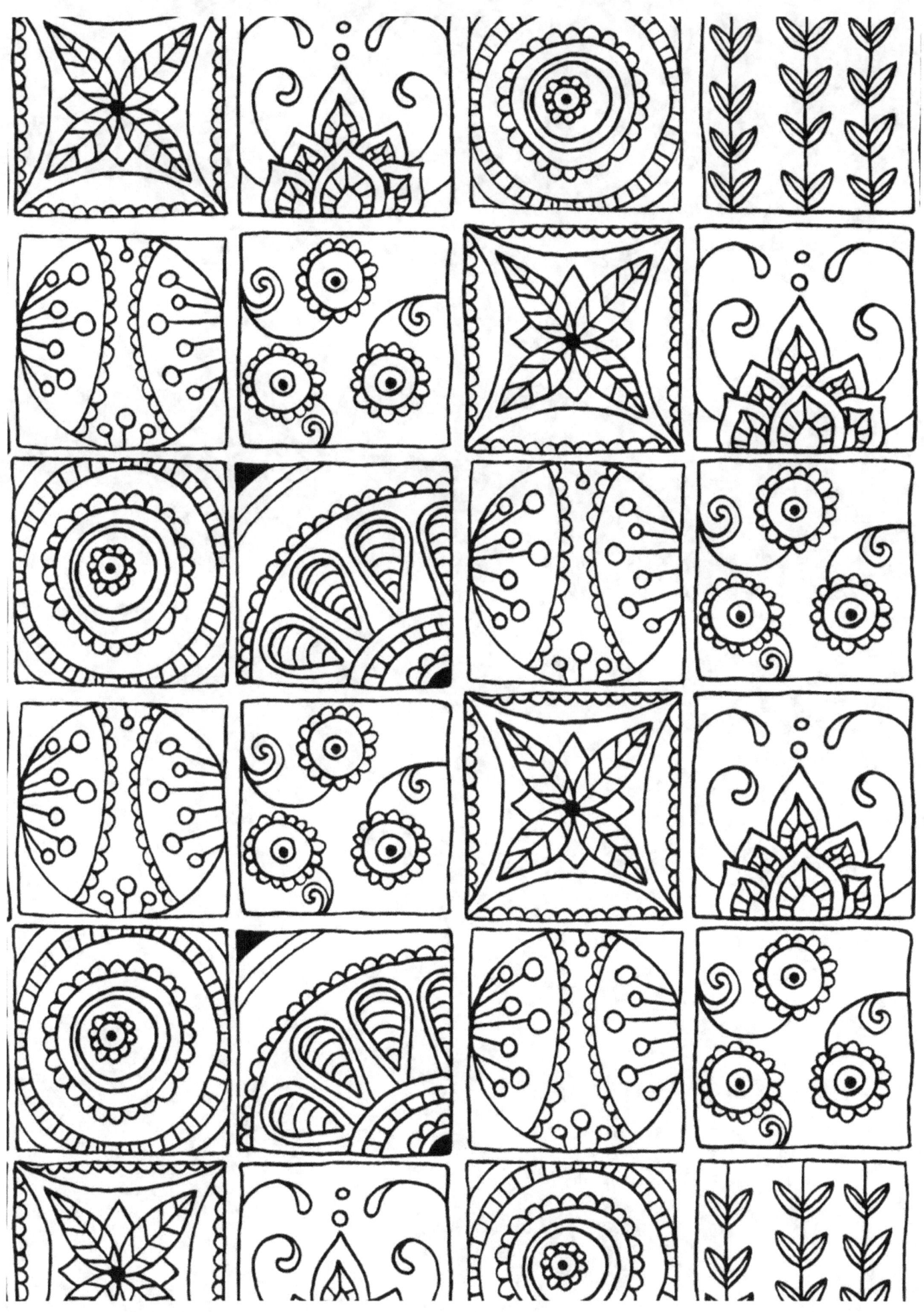

May Peace be your gift at Christmas and your blessing all year through!

Author unknown

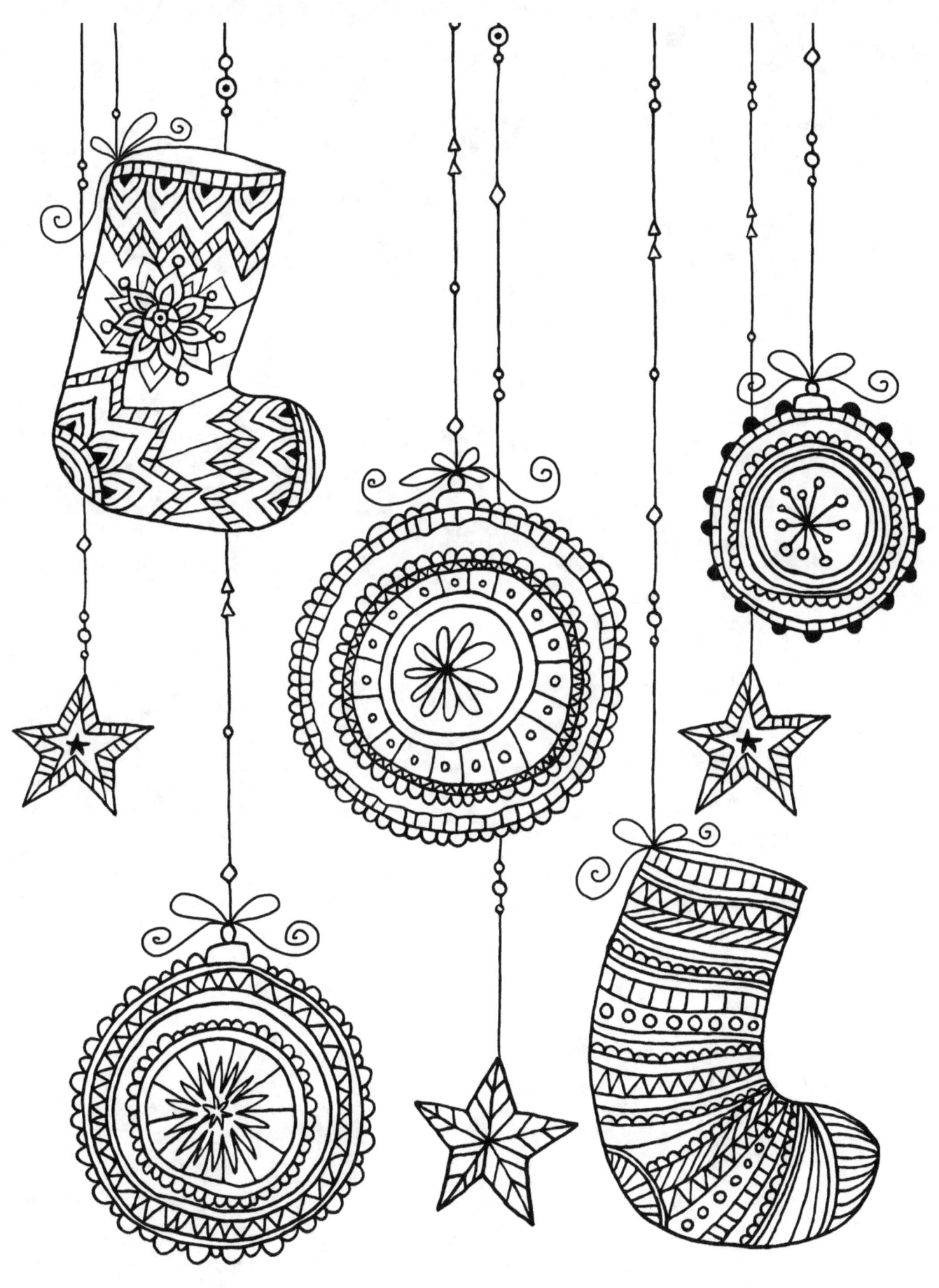

I will honor Christmas in my heart, and try to keep it all the year.

Charles Dickens

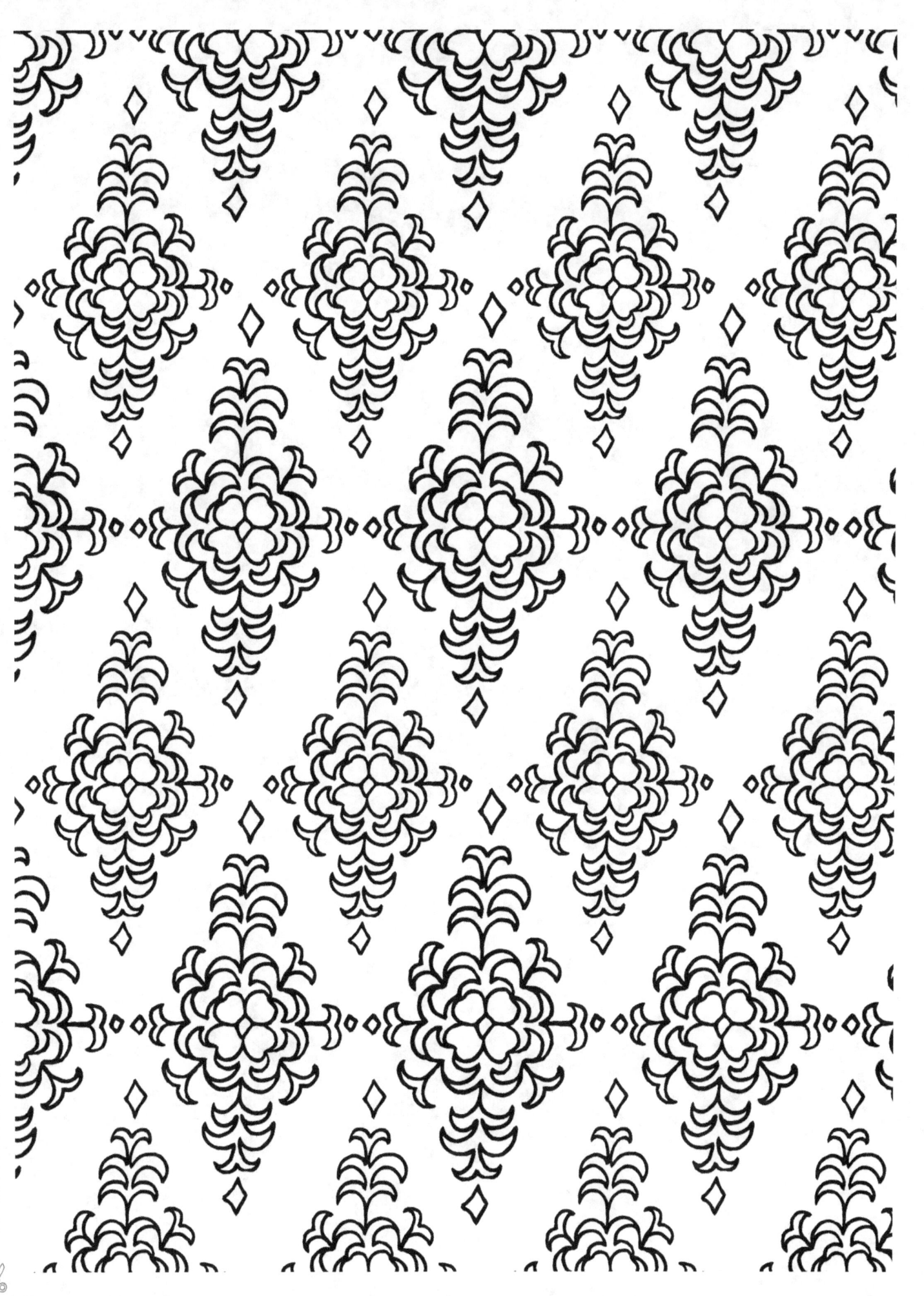

Never worry about the size of your Christmas tree. In the eyes of children, they are all 30 feet tall.

Larry Wilde

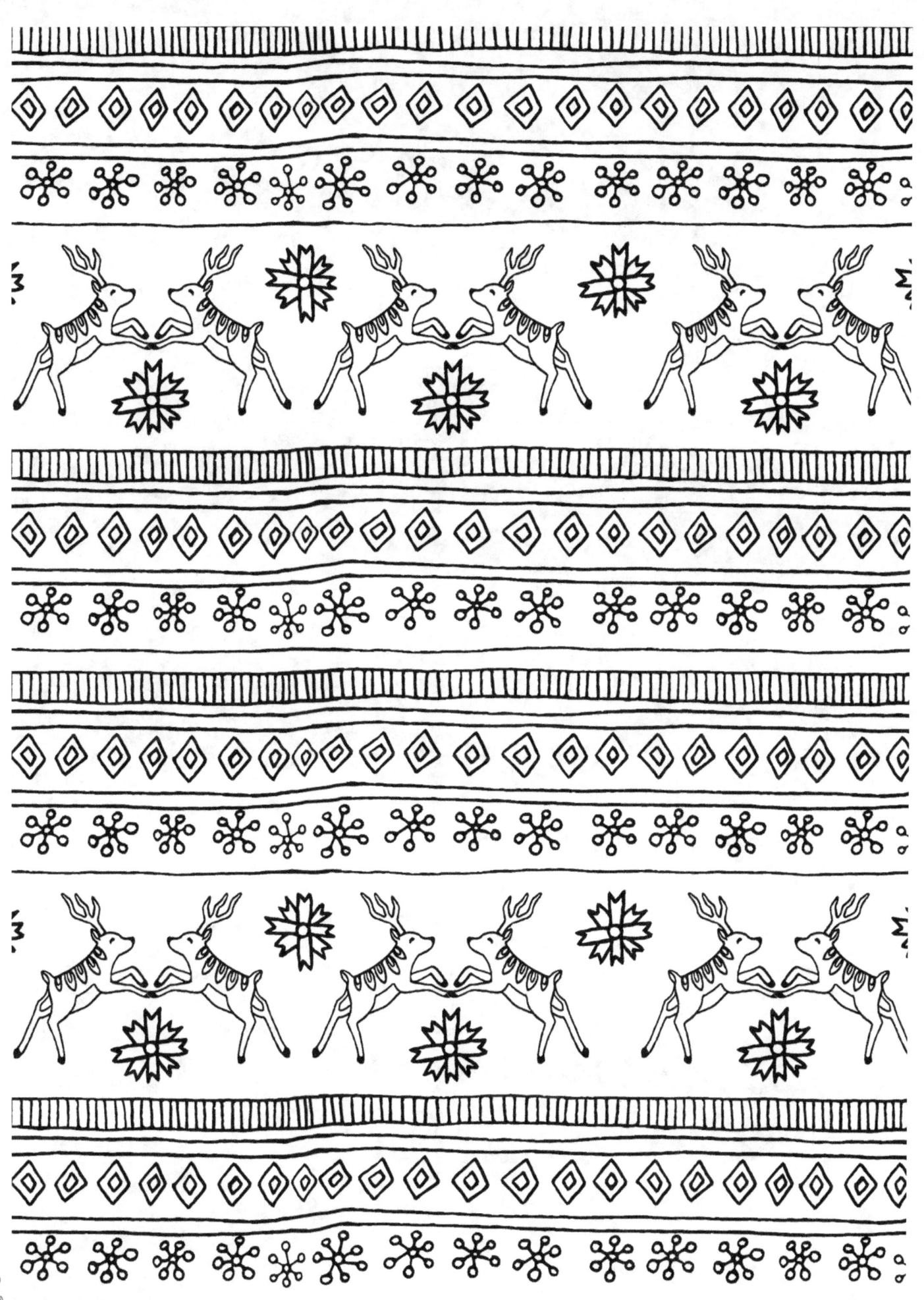

Christmas is the season for kindling the fire of hospitality in the hall, the genial flame of charity in the heart.

Washington Irving

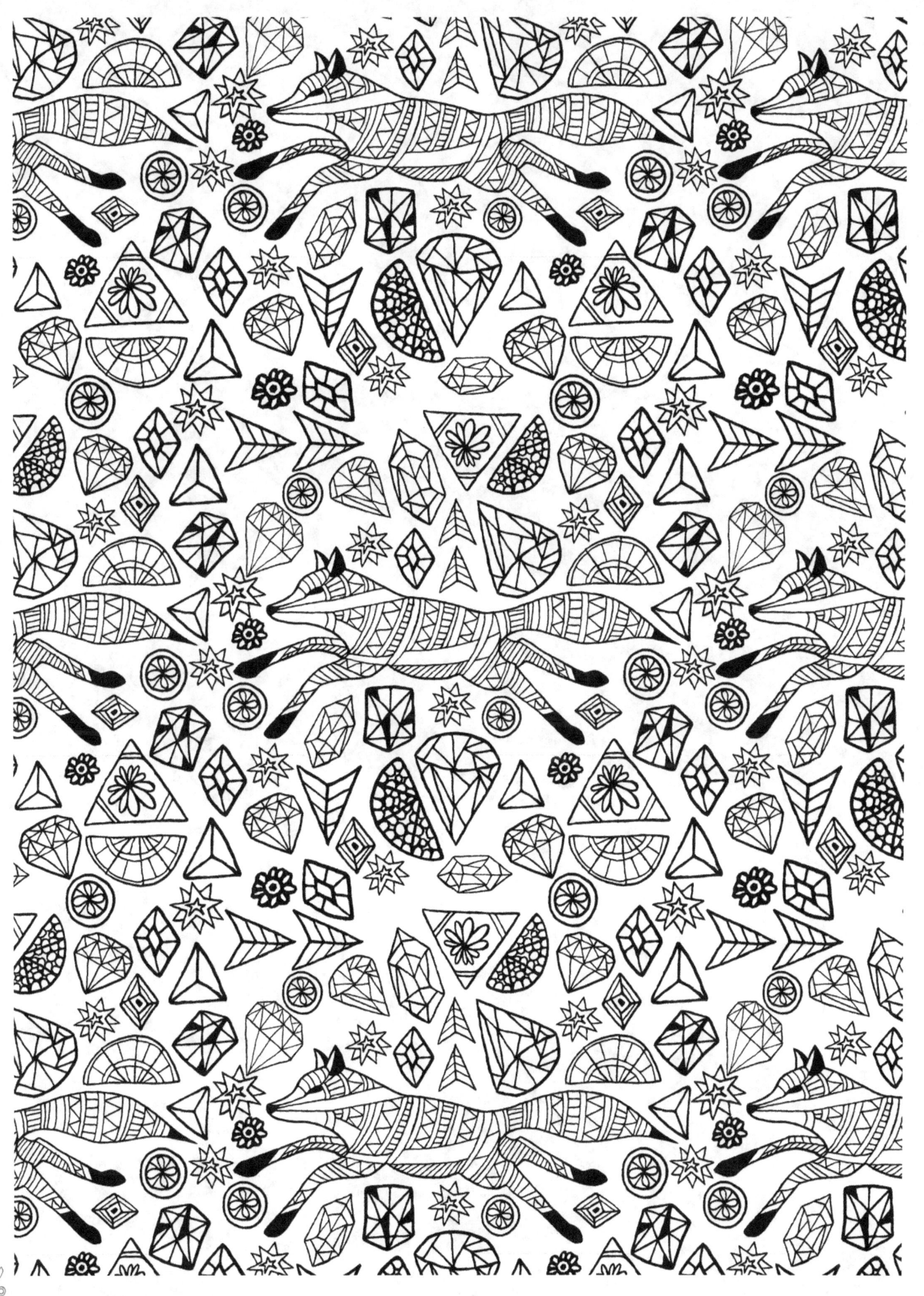

Gifts of time and love are surely the basic ingredients of a truly merry Christmas.

Peg Bracken

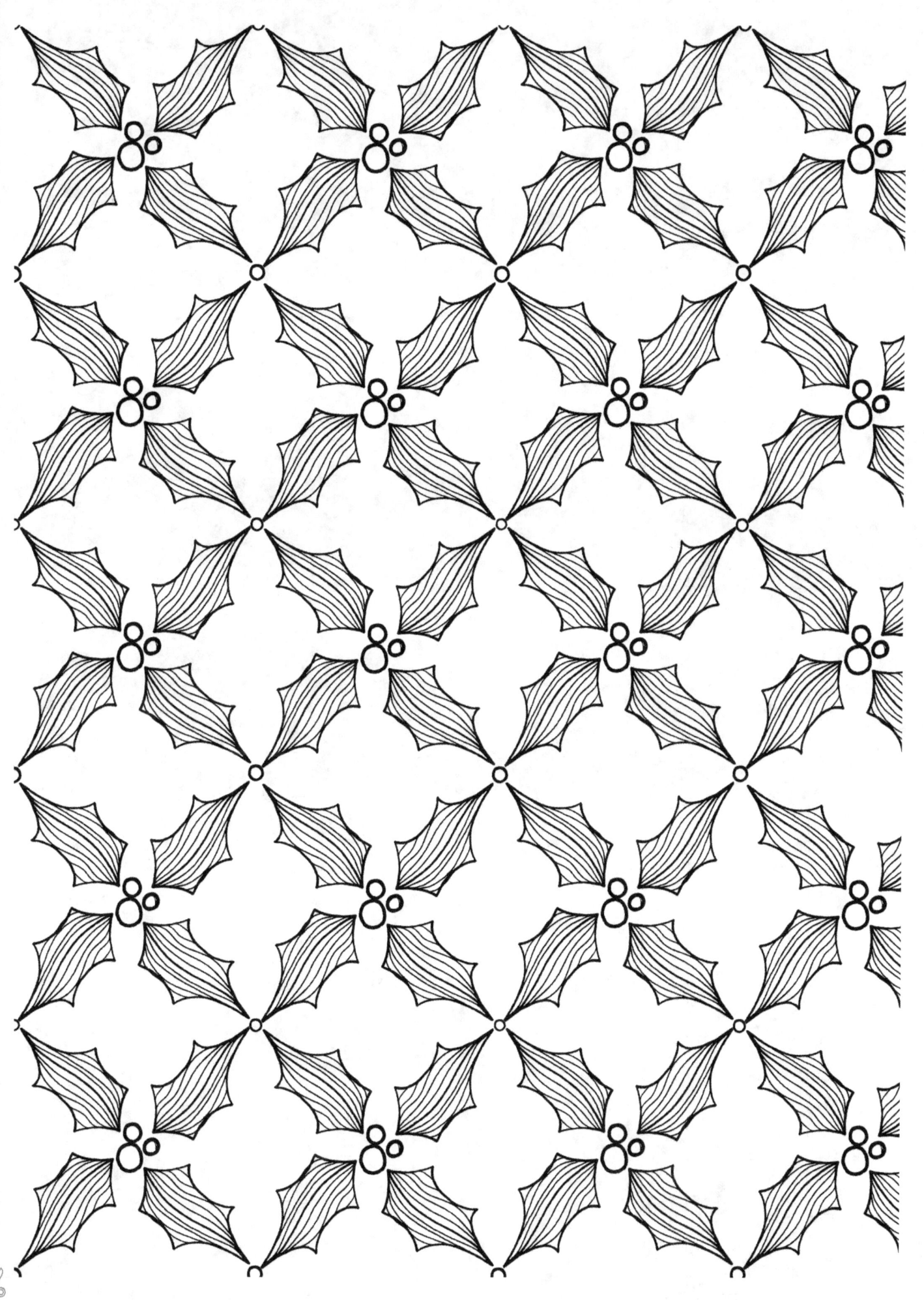

Blessed is the season which engages the whole world in a conspiracy of love!

Hamilton Wright Mabie

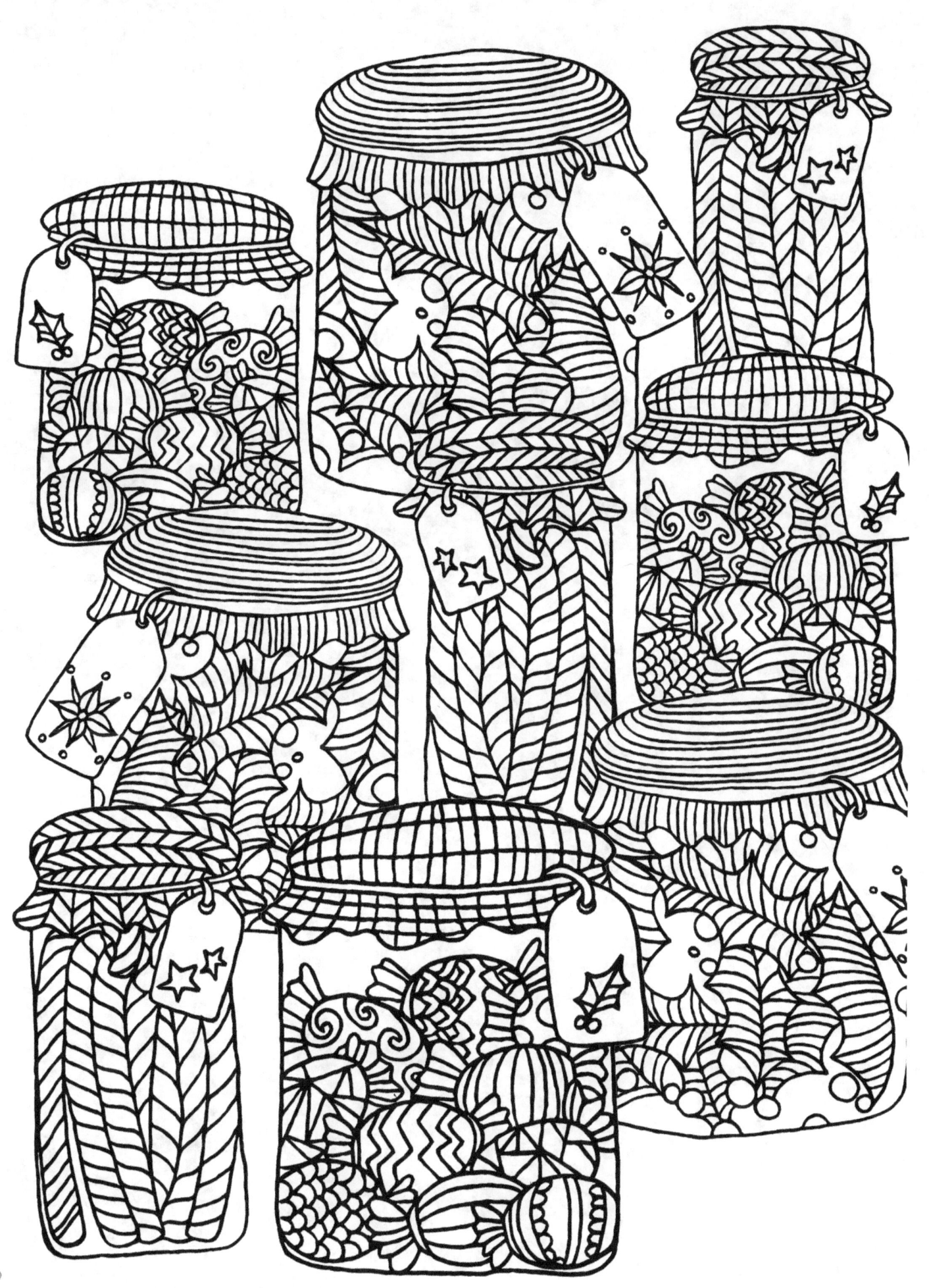

I wish we could put up some of the Christmas spirit in jars and open a jar of it every month.

Harlan Miller

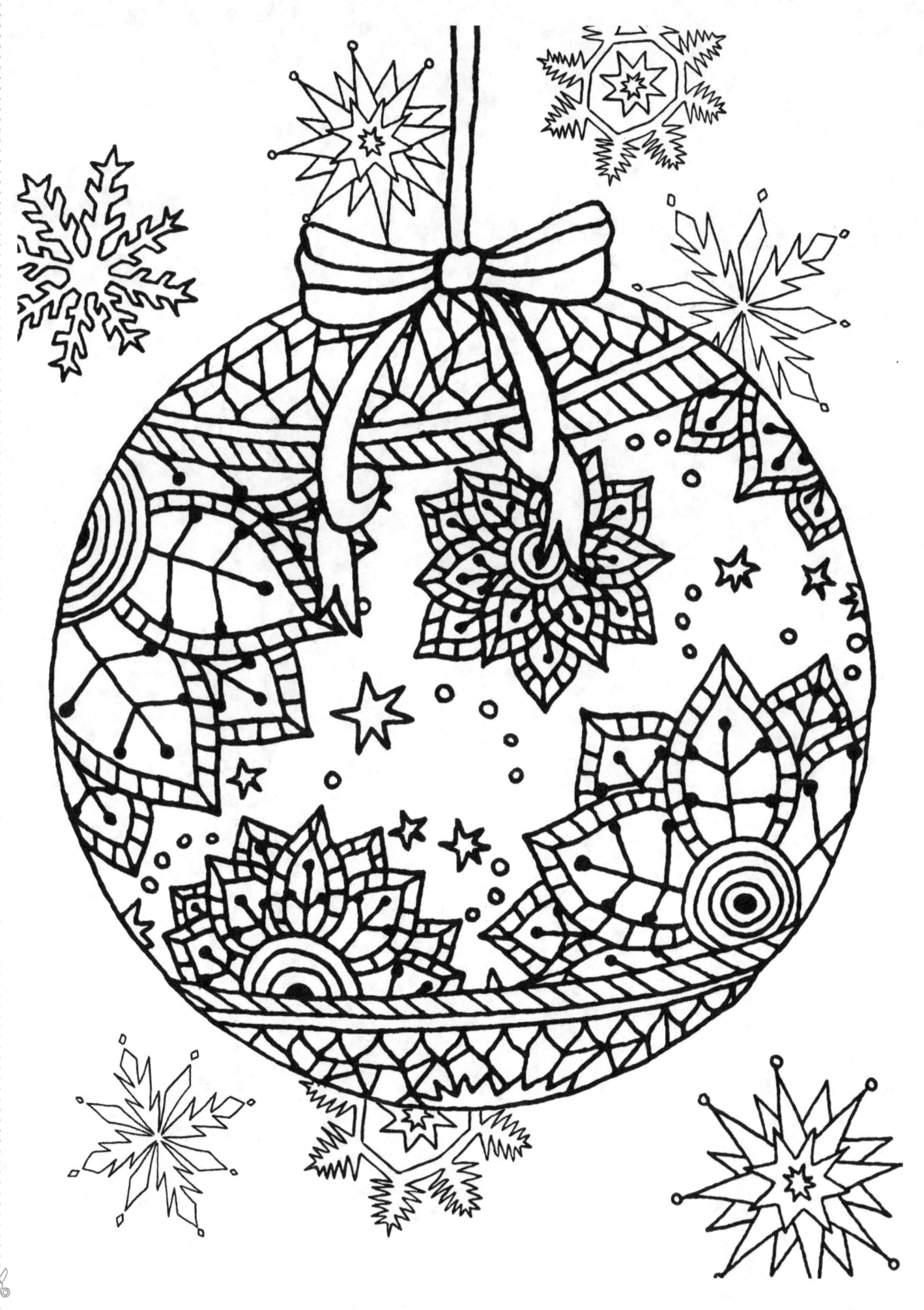

A Christmas candle is a lovely thing; It makes no noise at all, but softly gives itself away.

Eva Logue

Christmas is not as much about opening our presents as opening our hearts.

Janice Maeditere

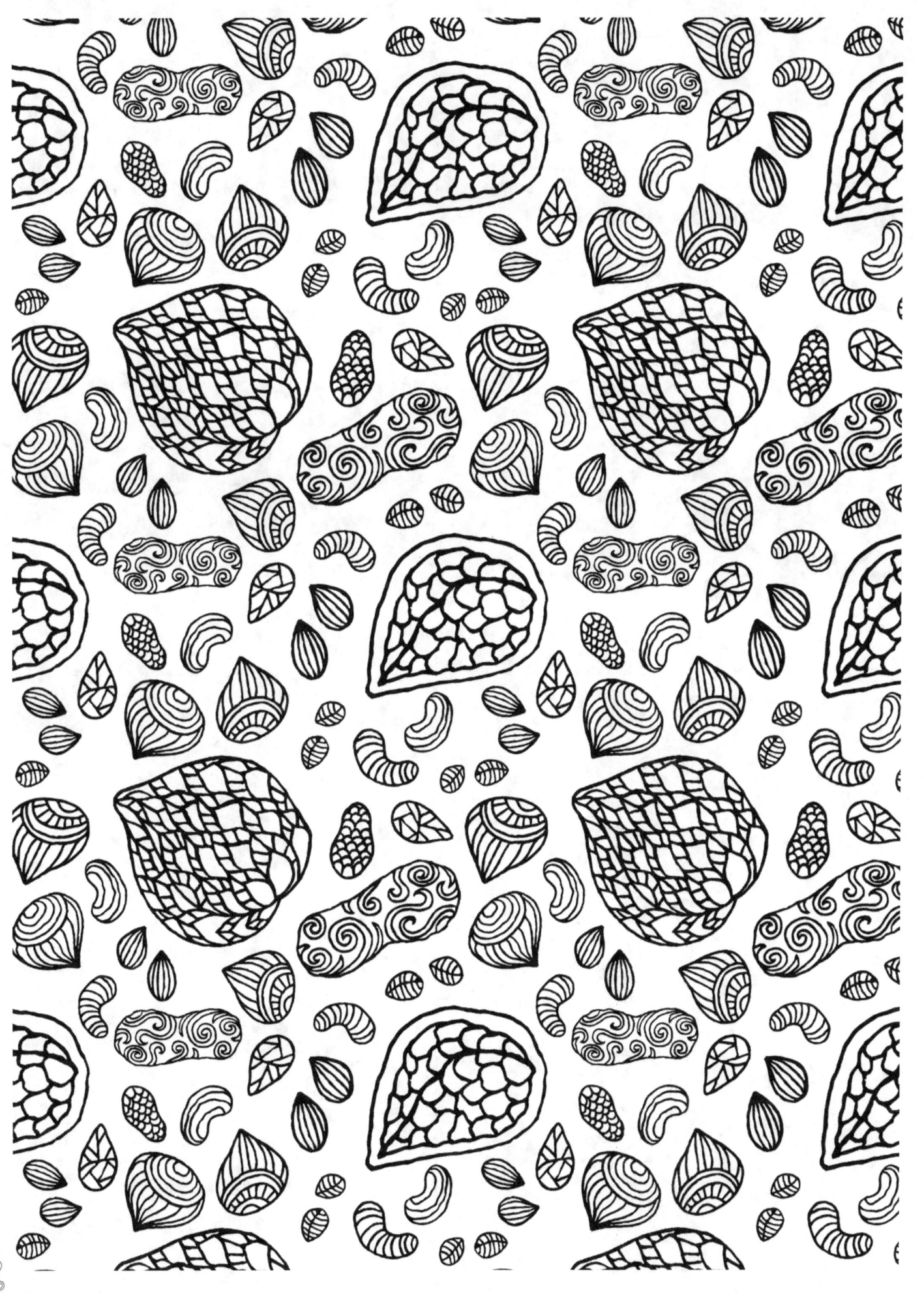

At Christmas play and make good cheer, for Christmas comes but once a year

Thomas Tusser

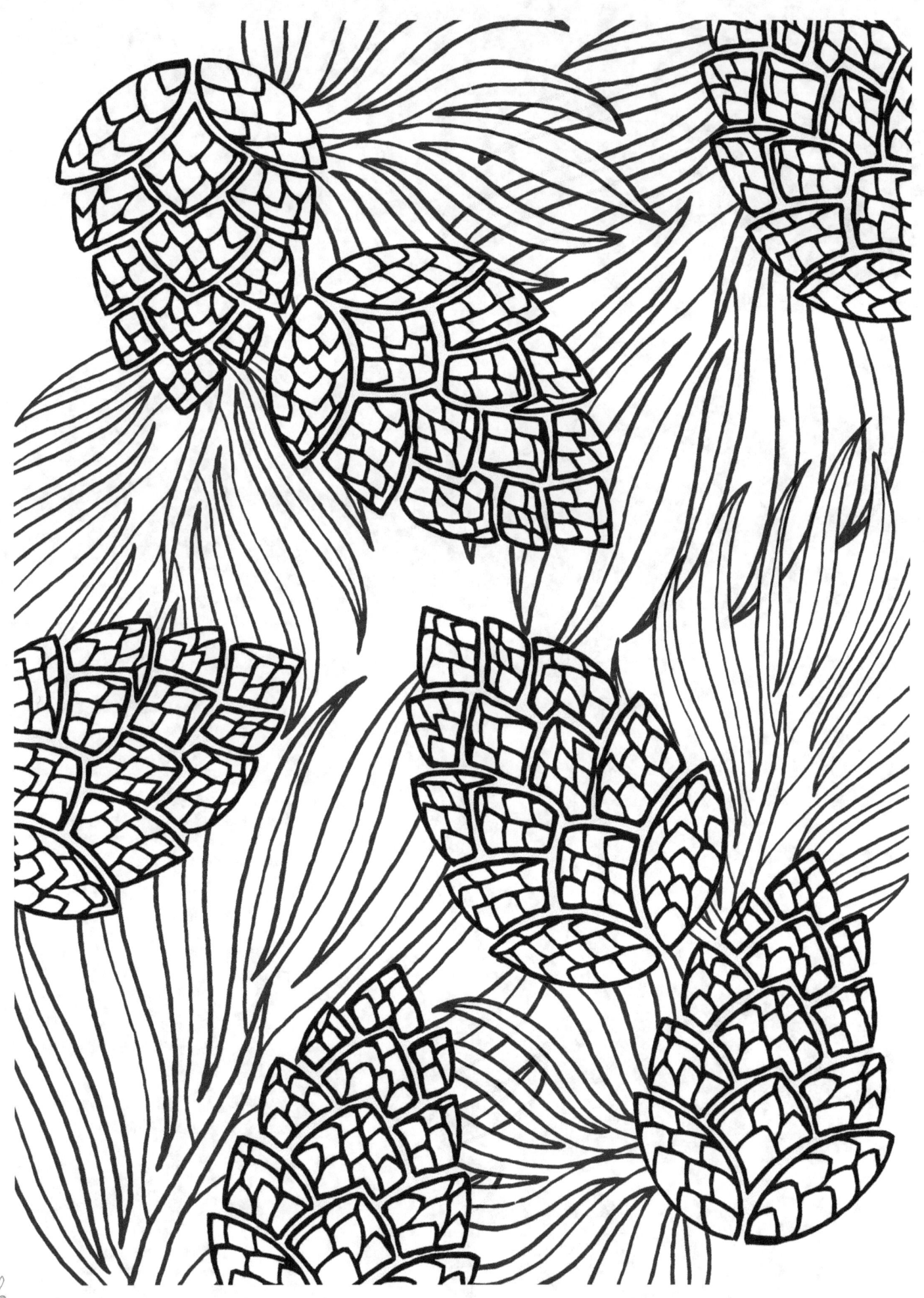

It is the Christmas time: And up and down 'twixt heaven and earth, in glorious grief and solemn mirth, the shining angels climb.

Dinah Maria Mulock

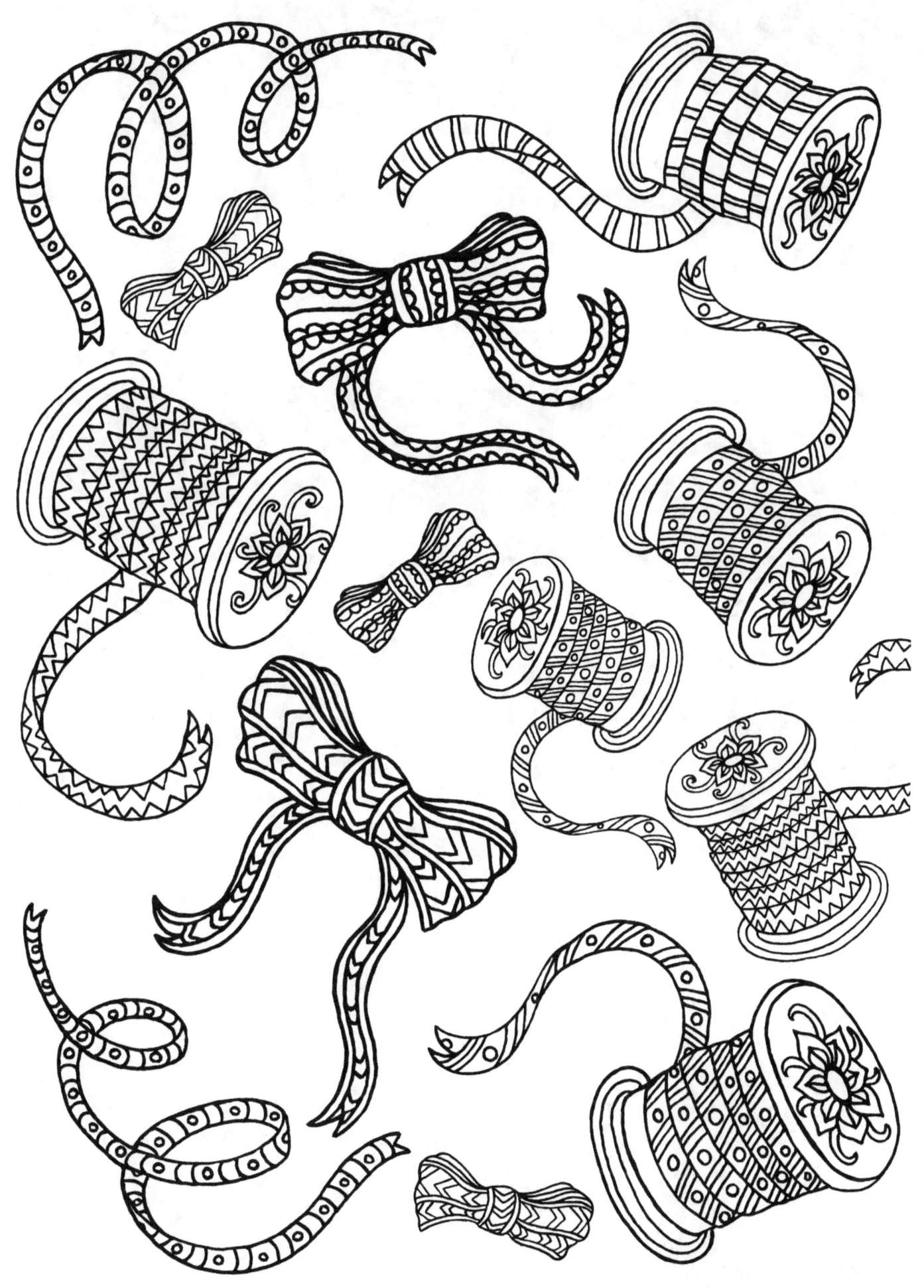

When we recall Christmas past, we usually find that the simplest things - not the great occasions - give off the greatest glow of happiness.

Bob Hope

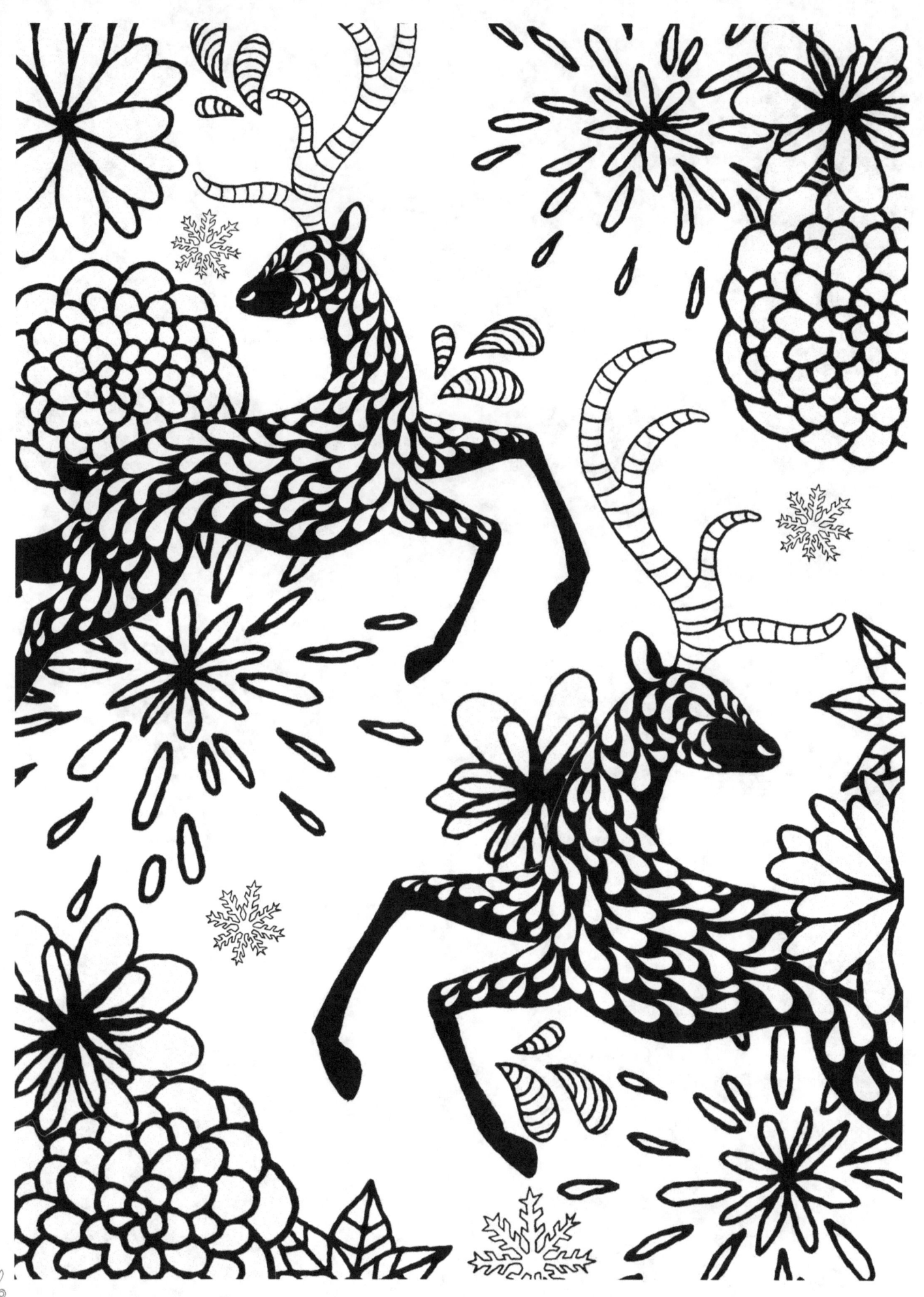

The best of all gifts around any Christmas tree: the presence of a happy family all wrapped up in each other.

Burton Hillis

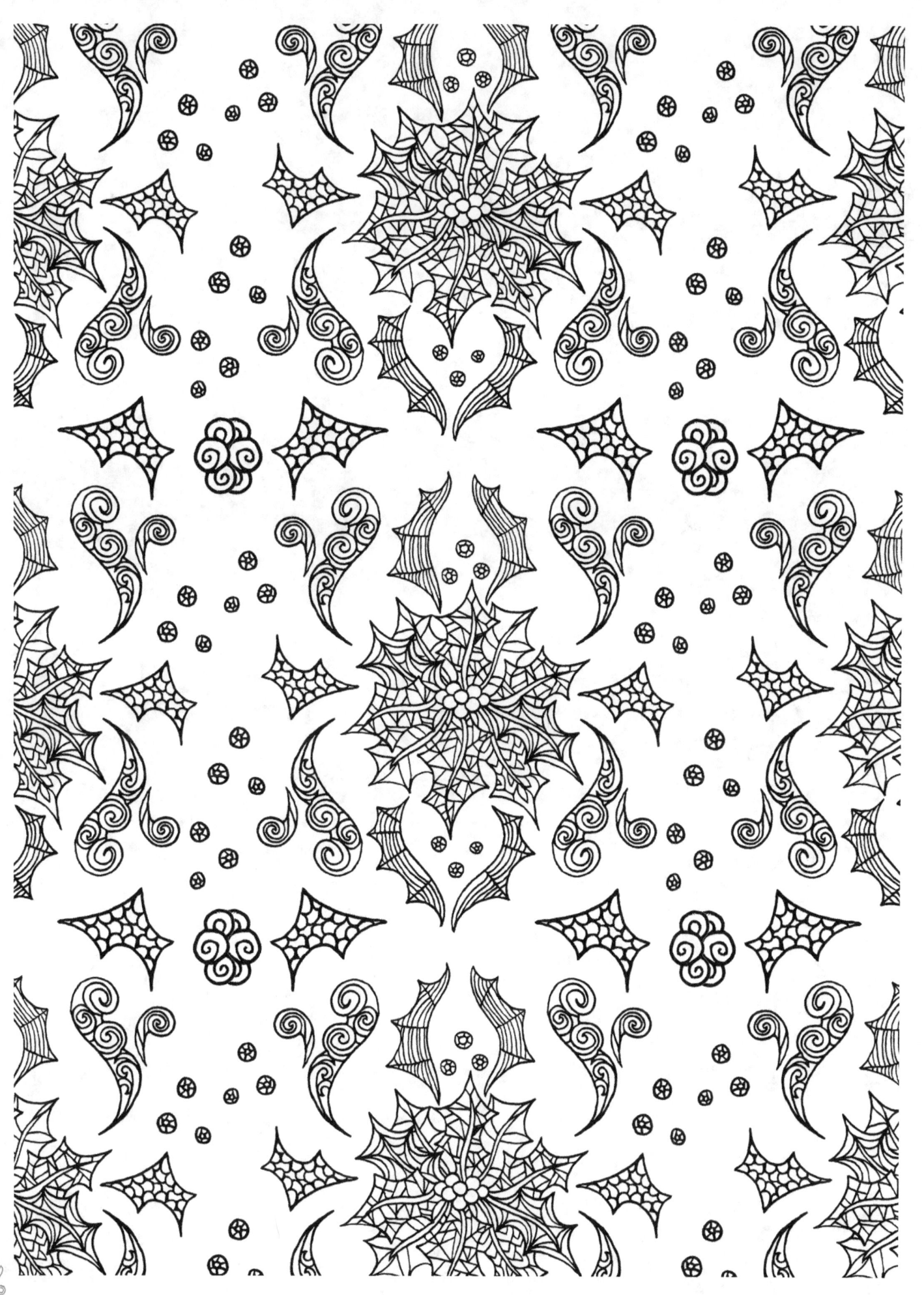

It's beginning to look a lot like Christmas; Soon the bells will start, and the thing that will make them ring is the carol that you sing right within your heart.

Meredith Willson

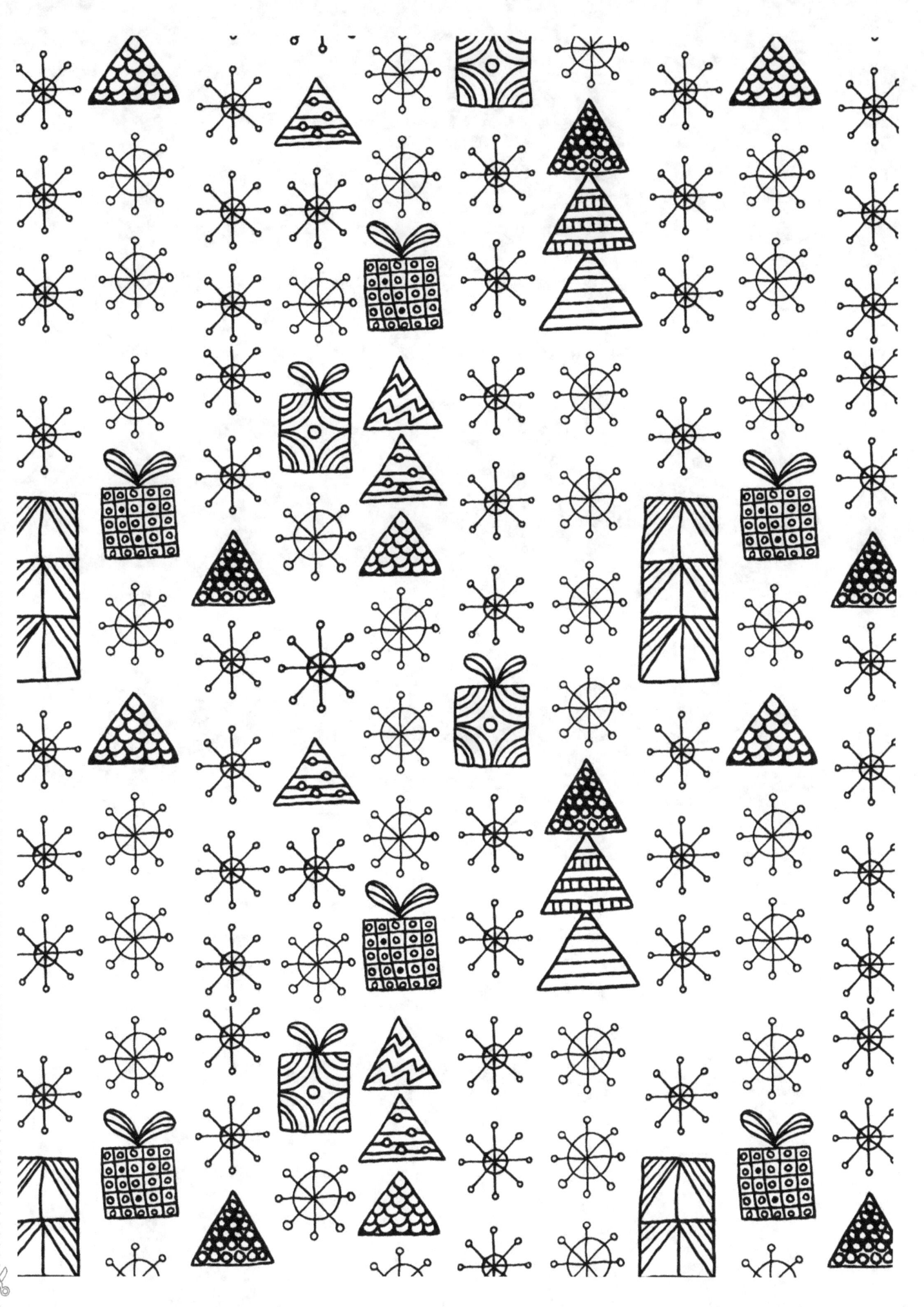

Christmas gift suggestions: to your enemy, forgiveness. To an opponent, tolerance. To a friend, your heart. To a customer, service. To all, charity. To every child, a good example. To yourself, respect.

Oren Arnold

Instead of being a time of unusual behavior, Christmas is perhaps the only time in the year when people can obey their natural impulses and express their true sentiments without feeling self-conscious and, perhaps, foolish. Christmas, in short, is about the only chance a man has to be himself.

Francis C. Farley

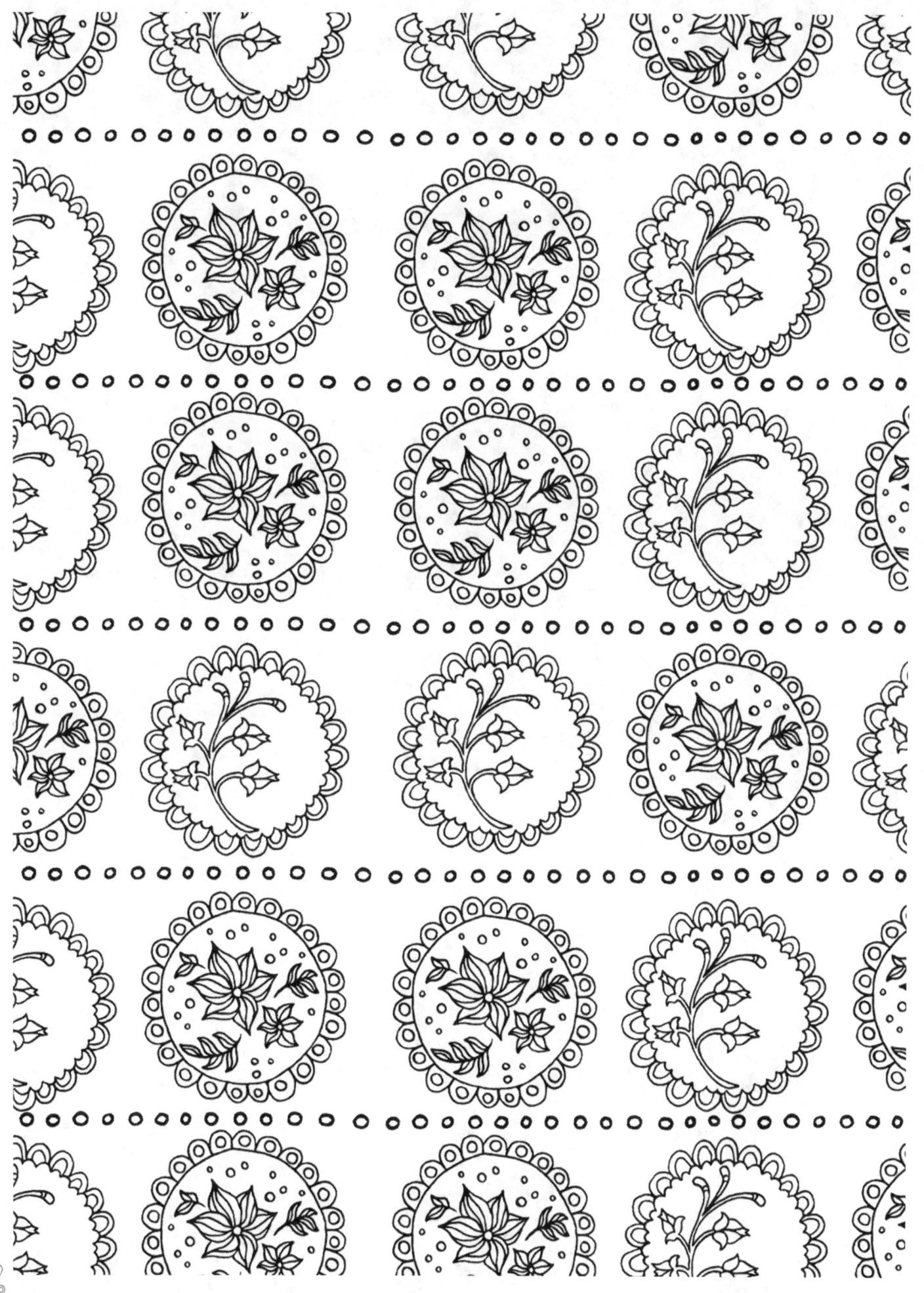

Christmas now surrounds us, Happiness is everywhere Our hands are busy with many tasks As carols fill the air.

Shirley Sallay

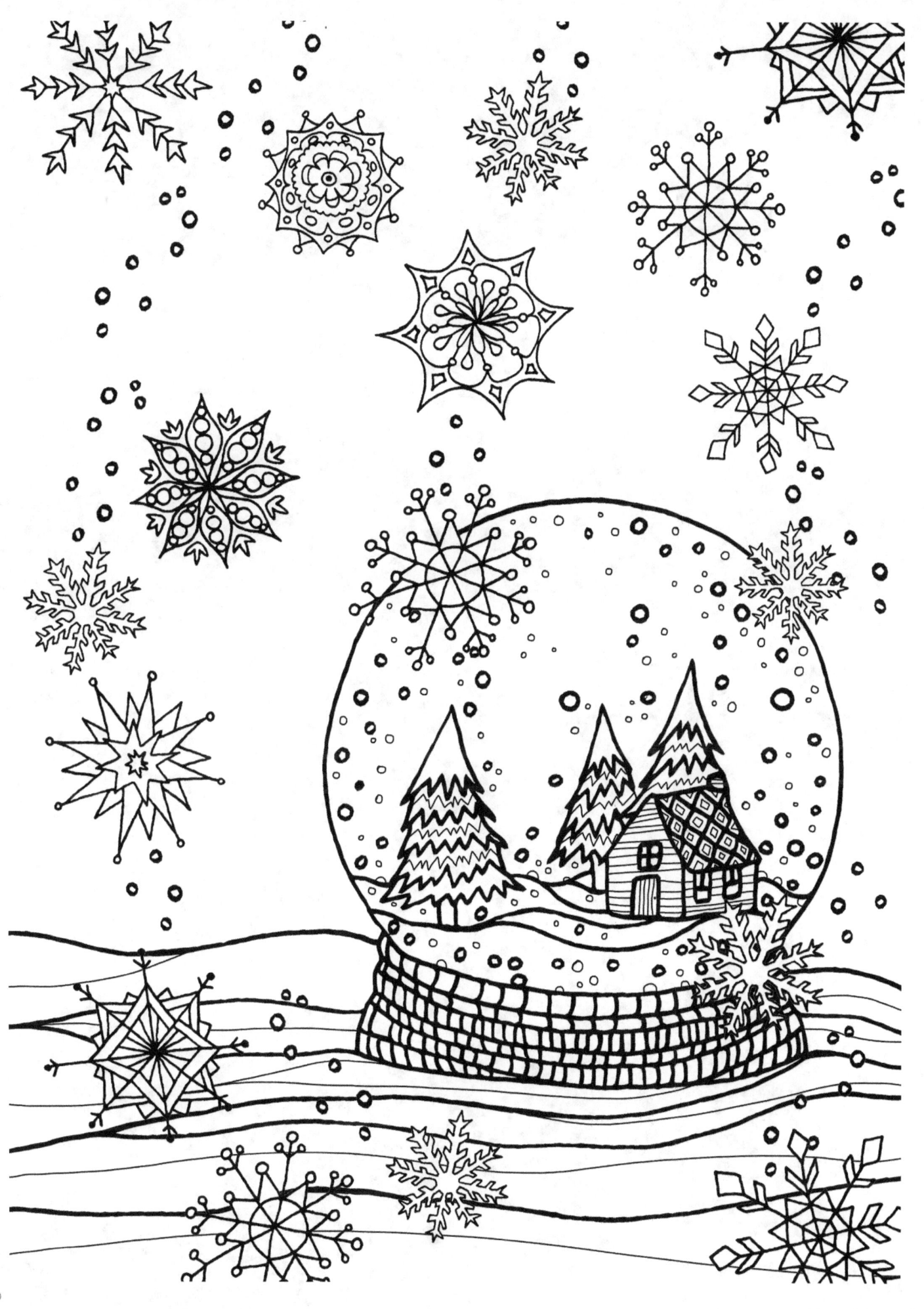

Each sight, each sound of Christmas and fragrances sublime make hearts and faces happy this glorious Christmastime.

Carice Williams

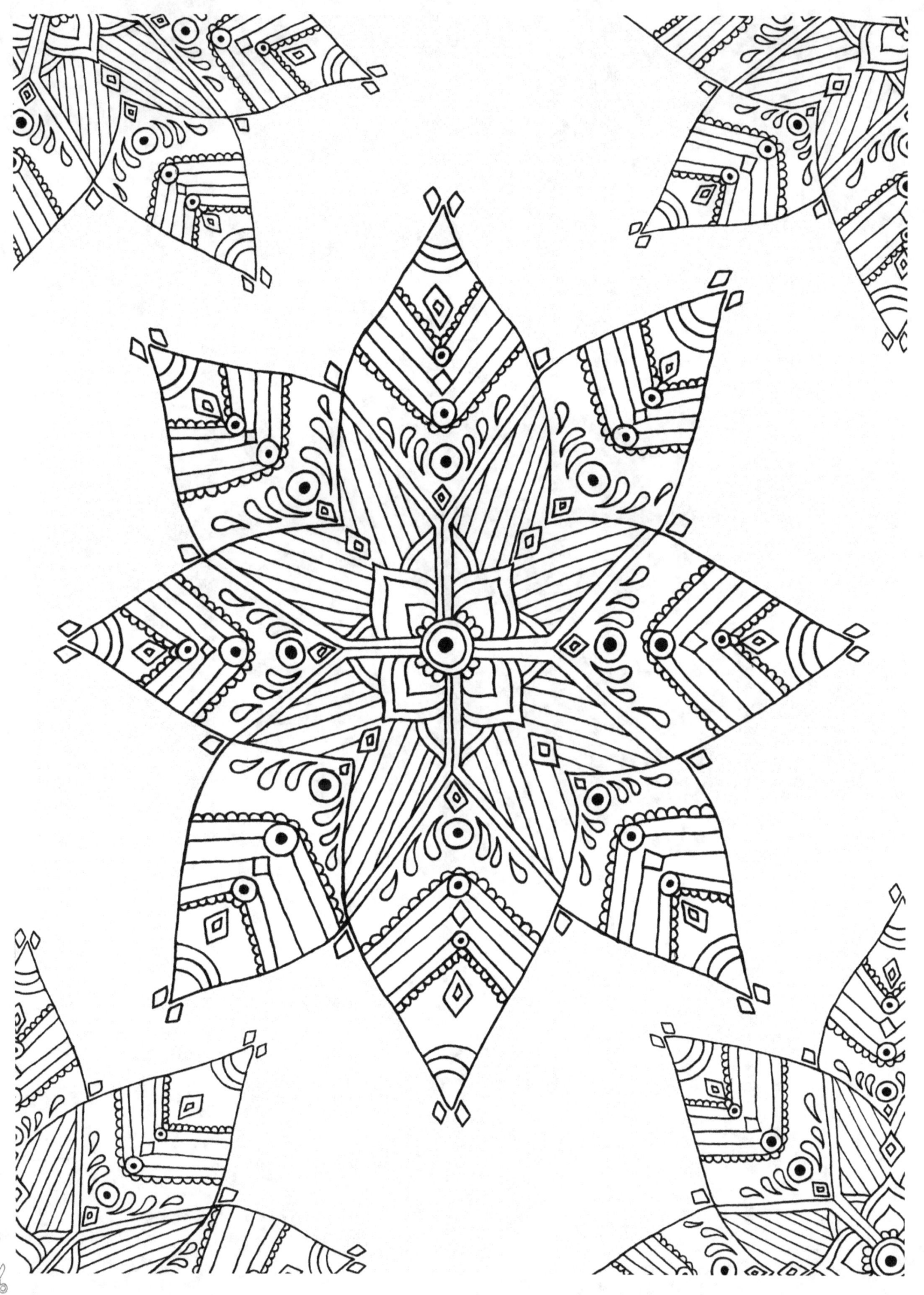

Good news from heaven the angels bring, Glad tidings to the earth they sing: To us this day a child is given, To crown us with the joy of heaven.

Martin Luther

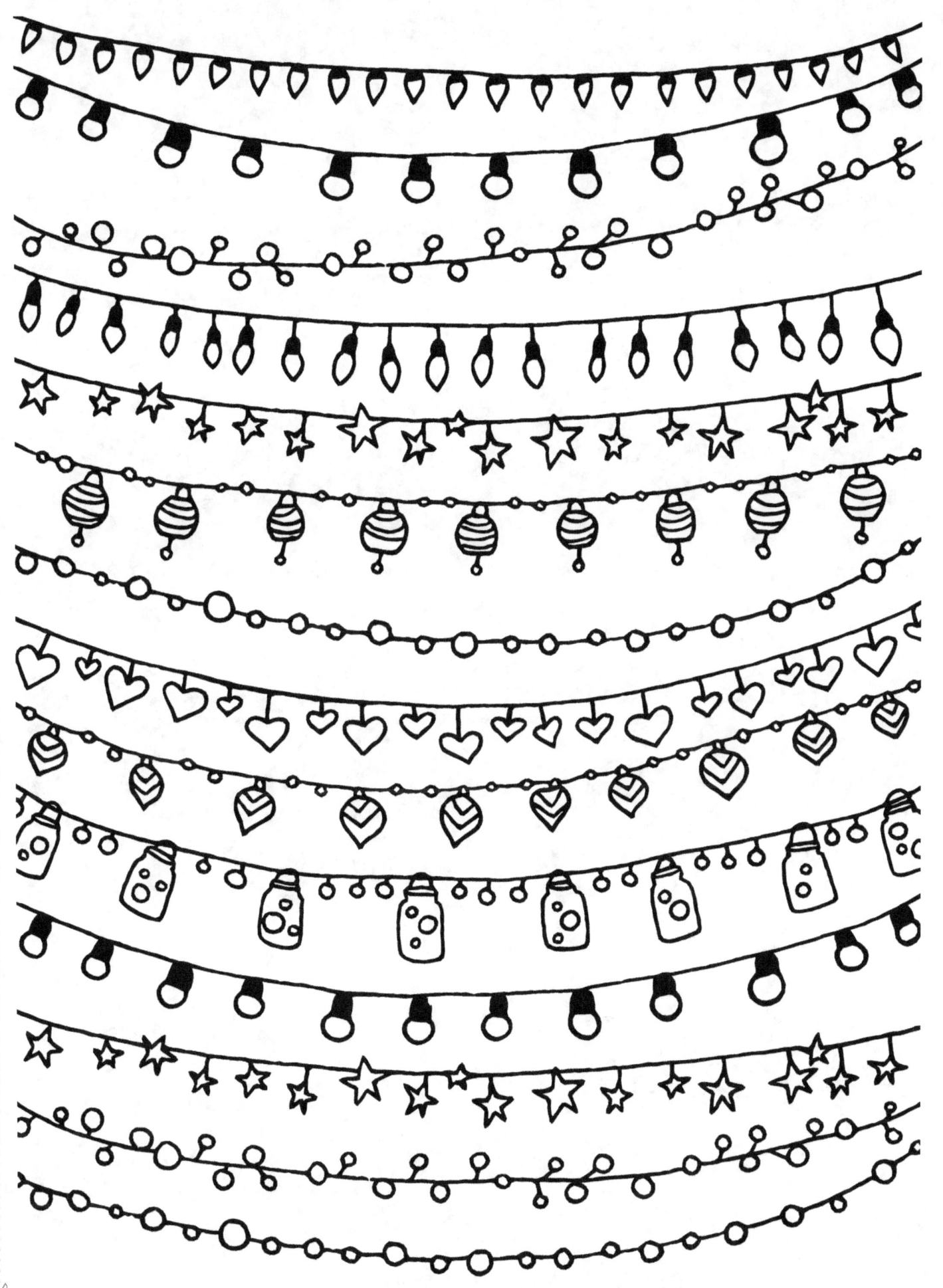

For centuries men have kept an appointment with Christmas. Christmas means fellowship, feasting, giving and receiving, a time of good cheer, home.

W. J. Tucker

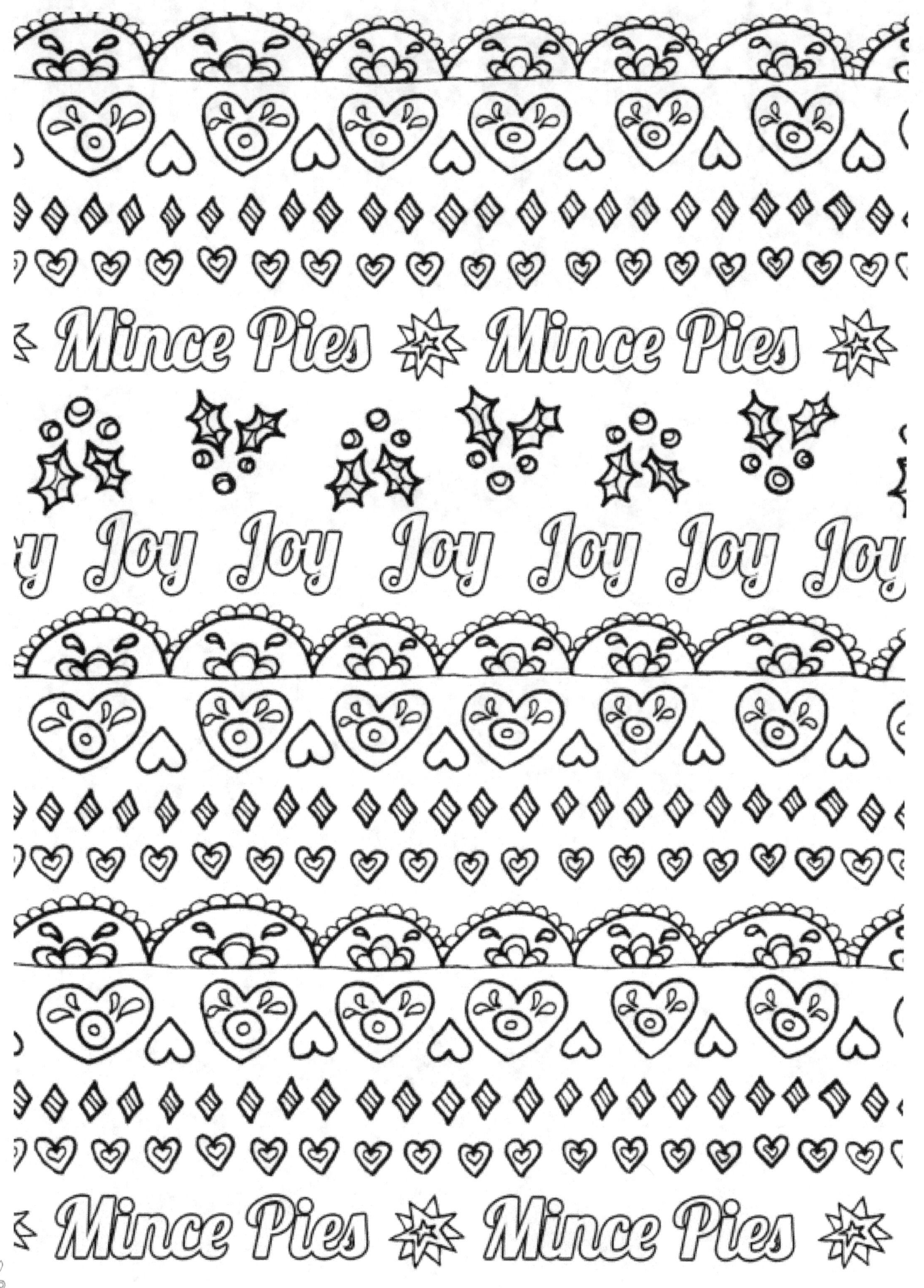

Christmas is not just a time for festivity and merry making. It is more than that. It is a time for the contemplation of eternal things. The Christmas spirit is a spirit of giving and forgiving.

J. C. Penney

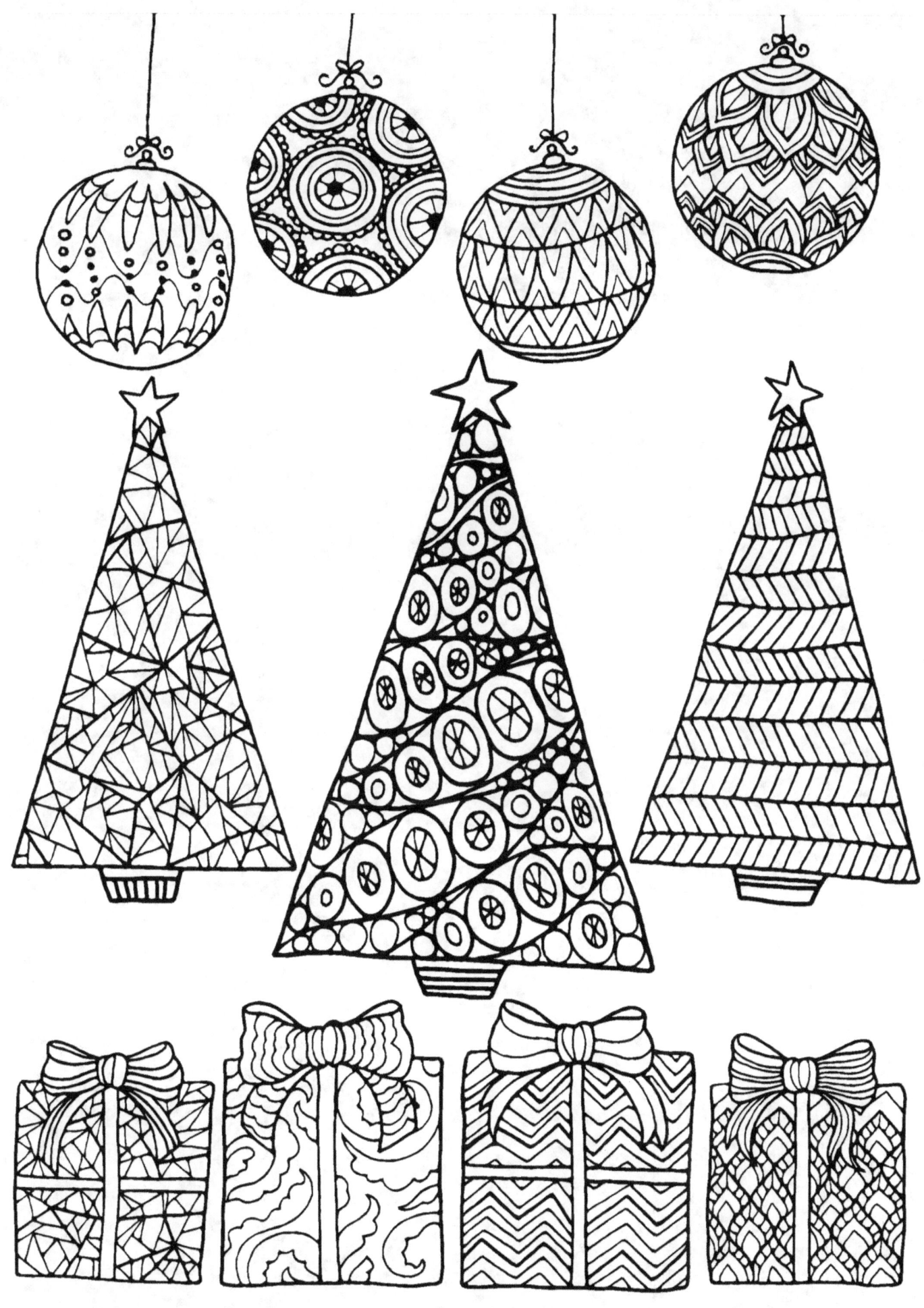

I heard the bells on Christmas Day their old, familiar carols play, and wild and sweet the words repeat of peace on earth, good-will to men!

Henry Wadsworth Longfellow

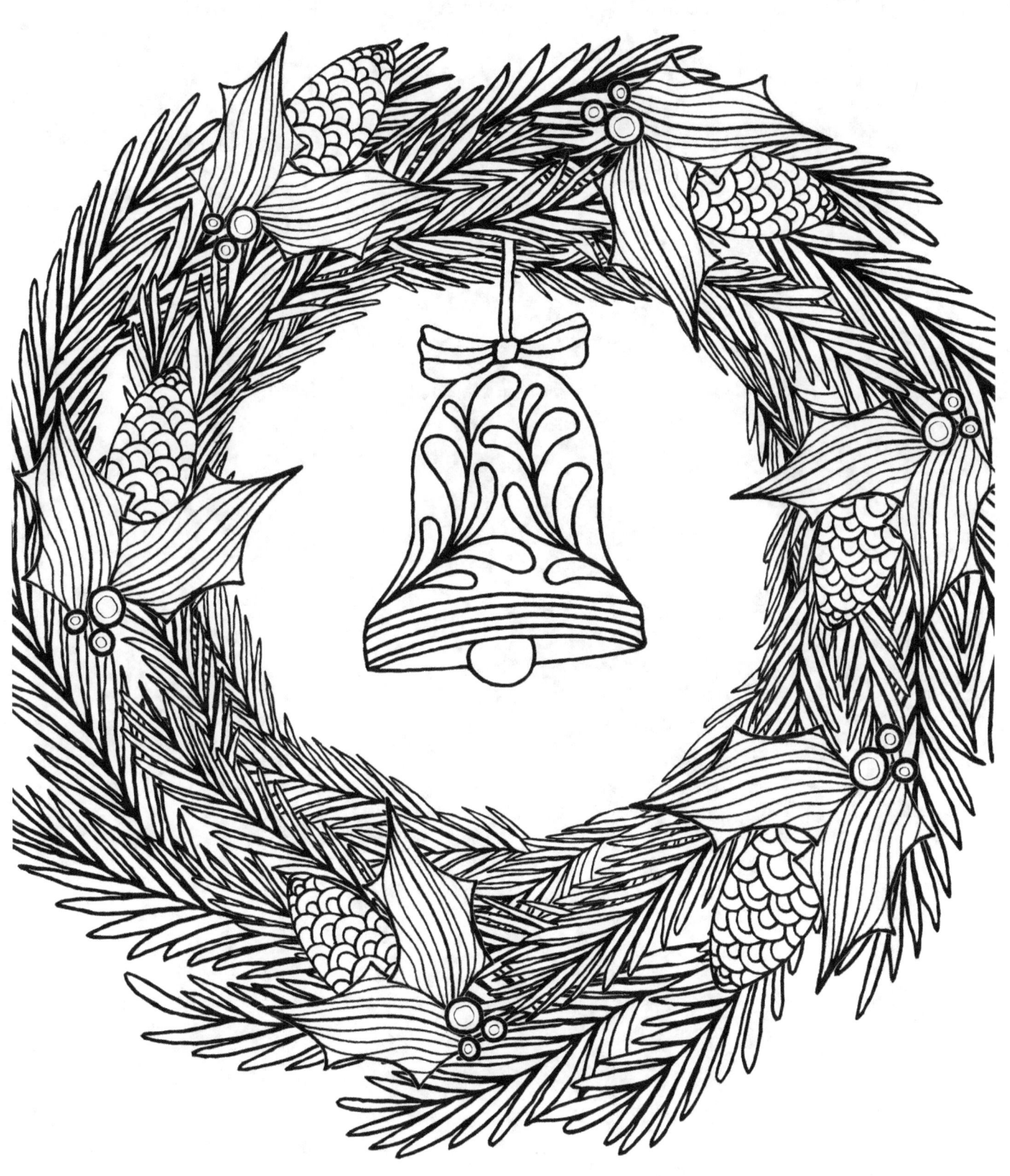

I love the Christmas-tide, and yet, I notice this, each year I live; I always like the gifts I get, But how I love the gifts I give!

Carolyn Wells

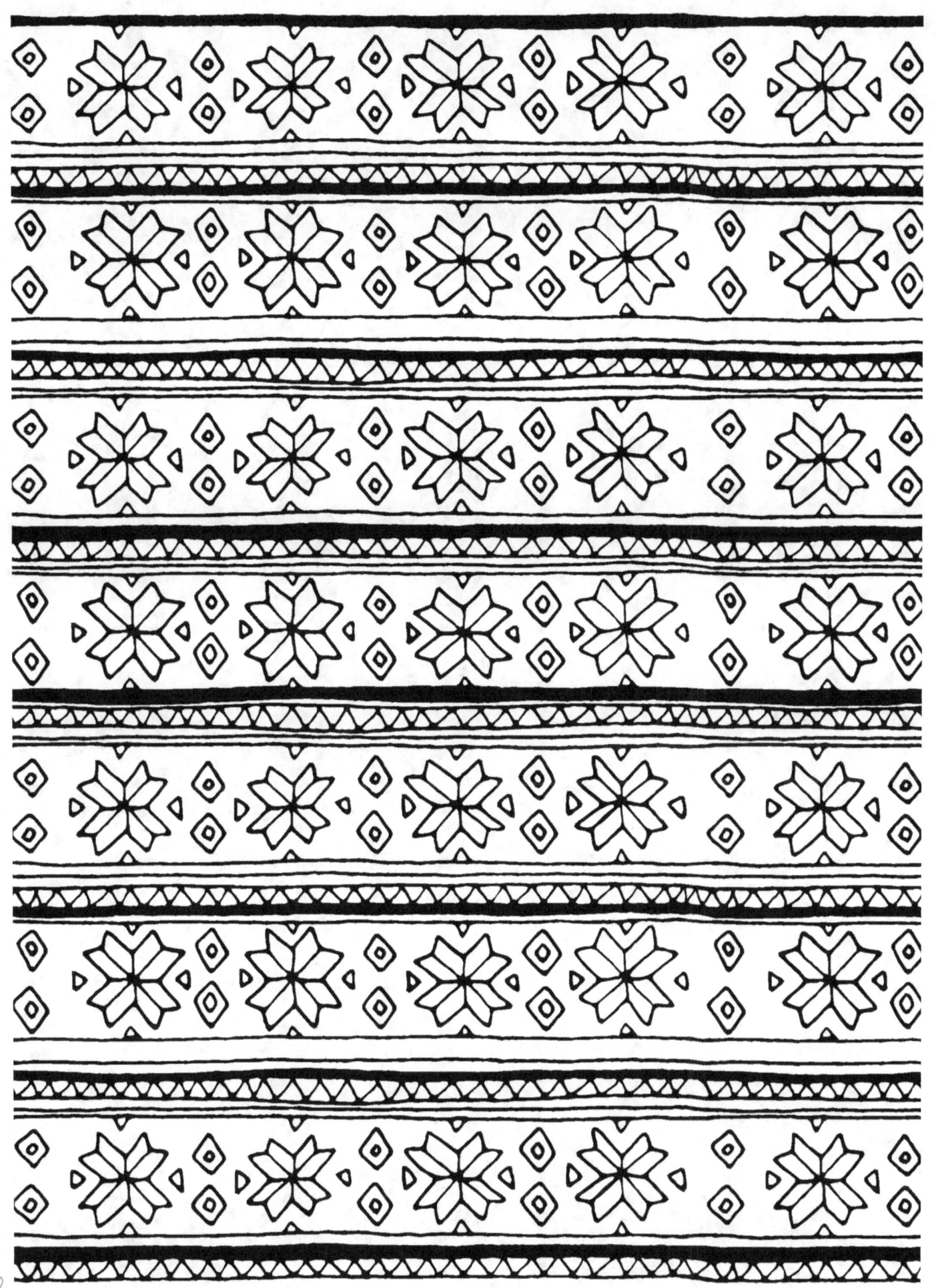

Let us have music for Christmas...Sound the trumpet of joy and rebirth; Let each of us try, with a song in our hearts, To bring peace to men on earth.

Mildred L. Jarrell

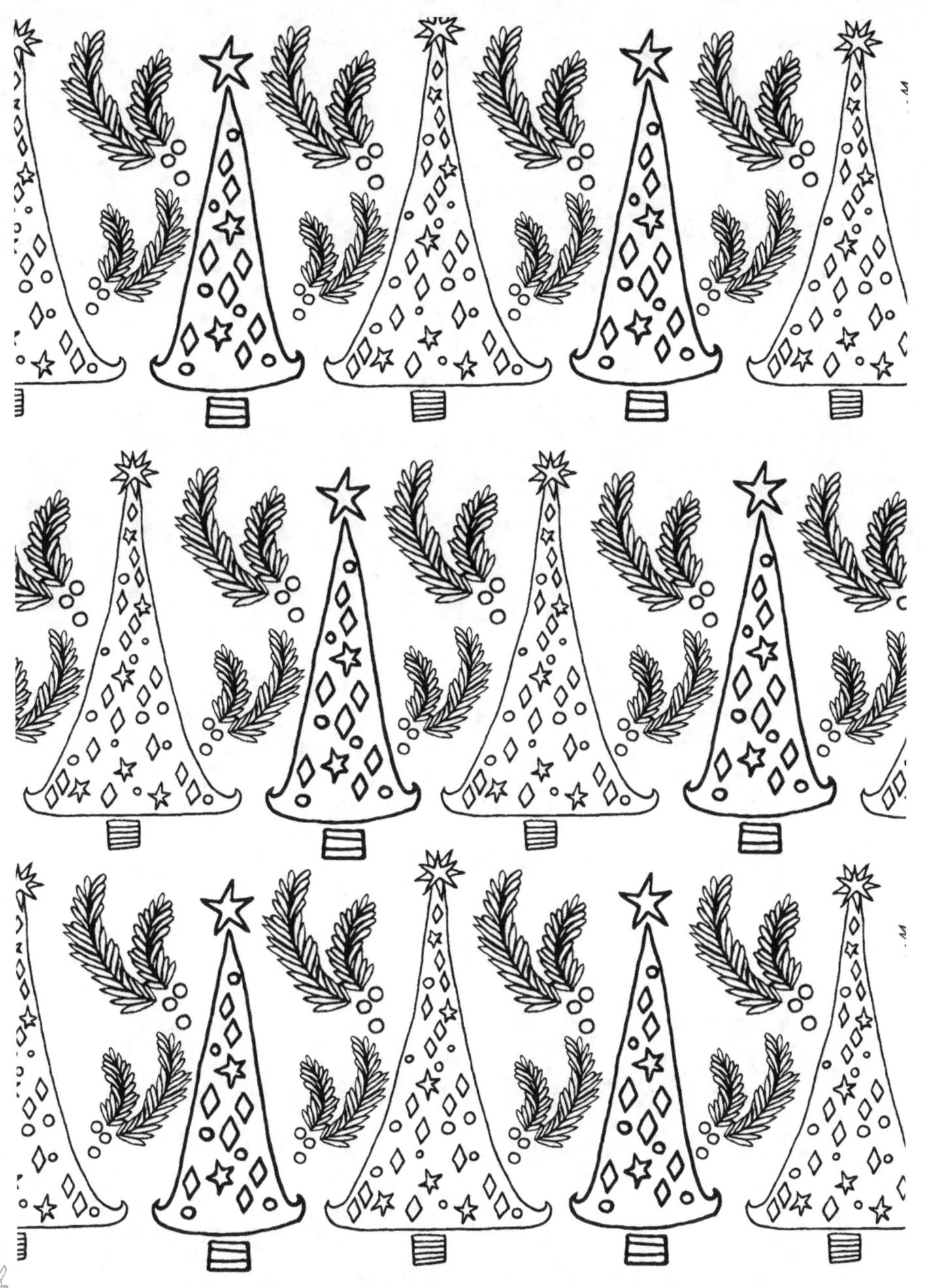

Christmas is not a time or a season but a state of mind. To cherish peace and good will, to be plenteous in mercy, is to have the real spirit of Christmas.

Calvin Coolidge

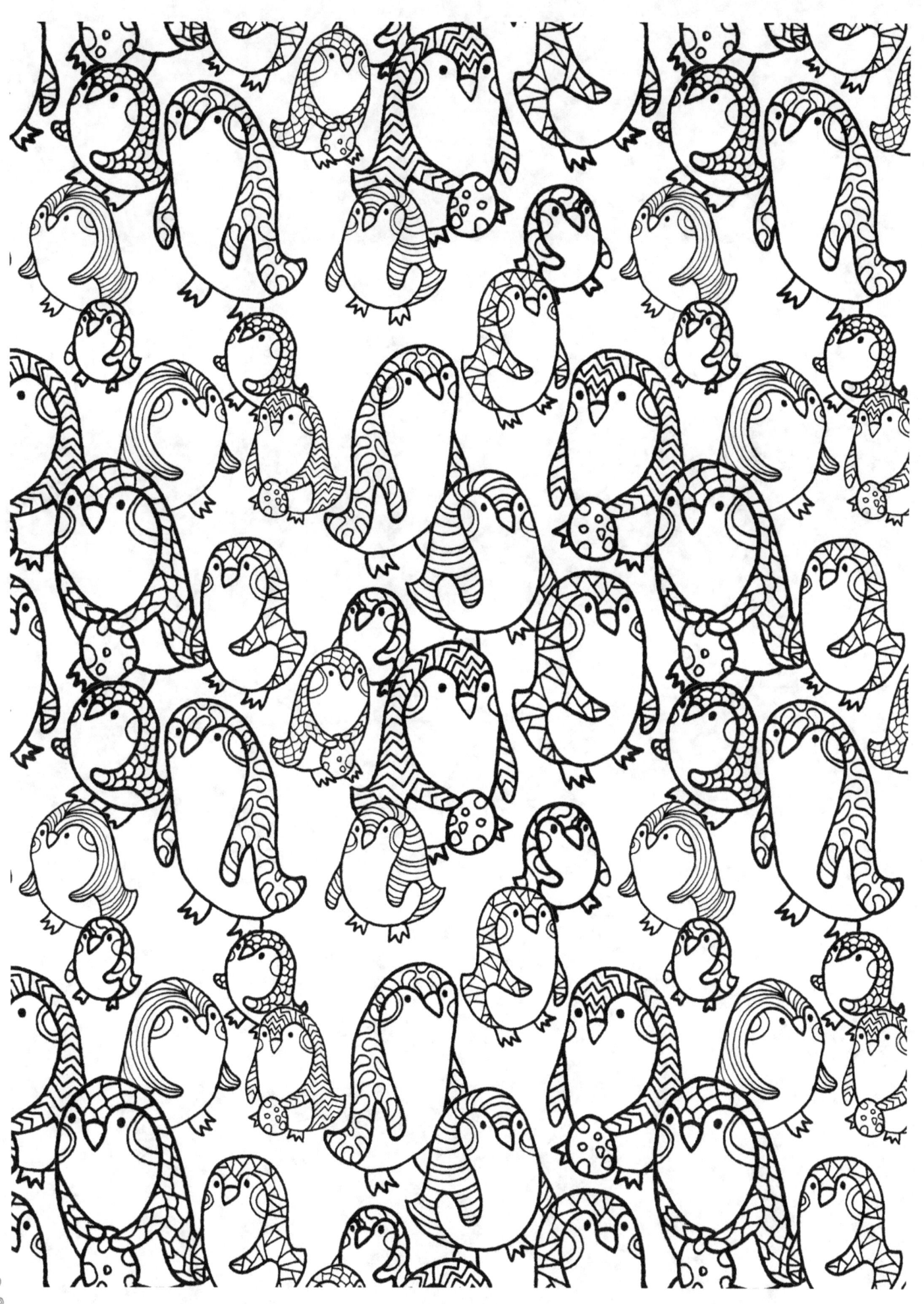

What is Christmas? It is tenderness for the past, courage for the present, hope for the future. It is a fervent wish that every path may lead to peace, and that every cup may overflow with blessings rich and eternal, and that every path may lead to peace.

Agnes M. Pharo

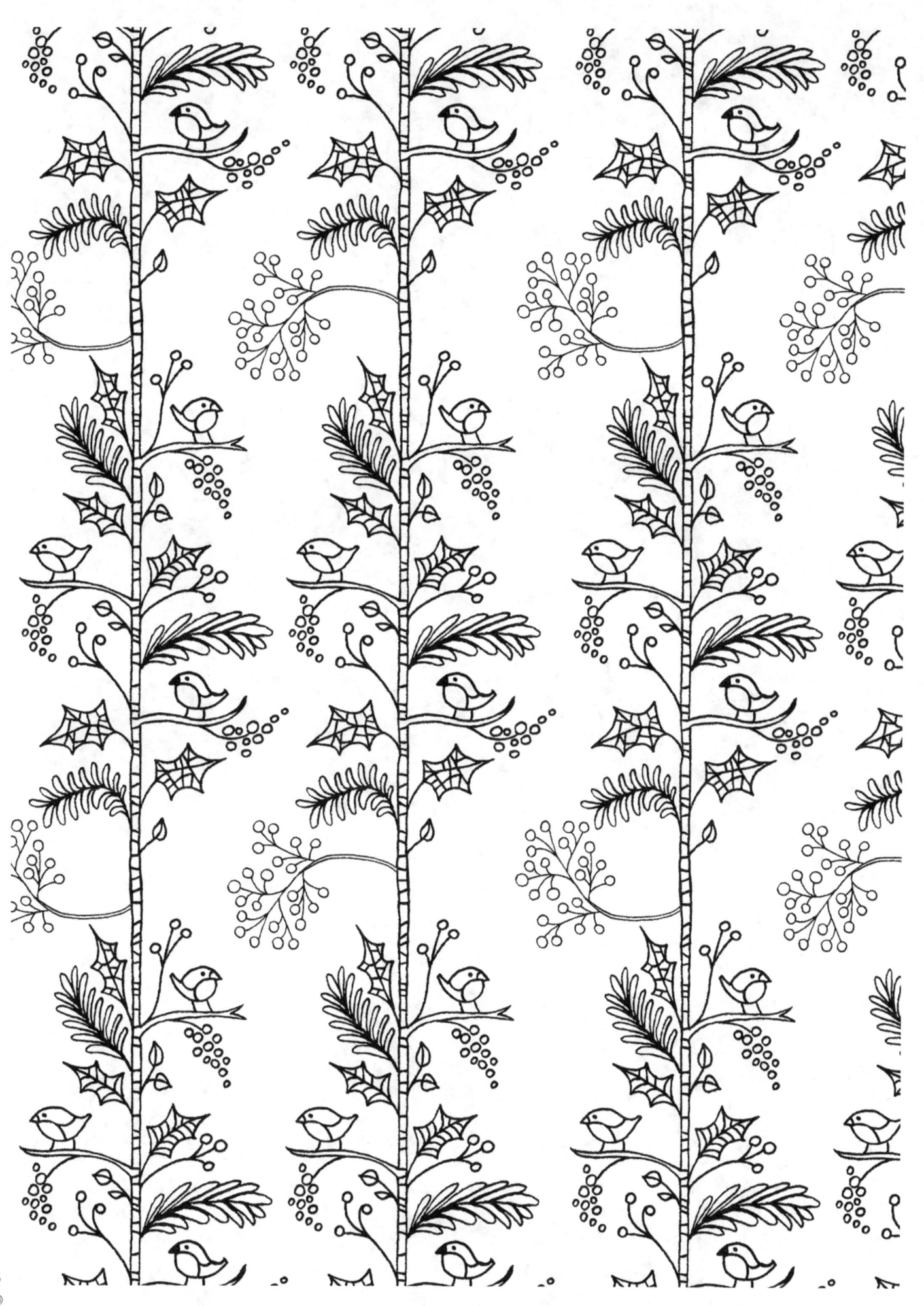

May Christmas lend a special charm to all you chance to do and may the season light your way to hopes and dreams anew.

Garnett Ann Schultz

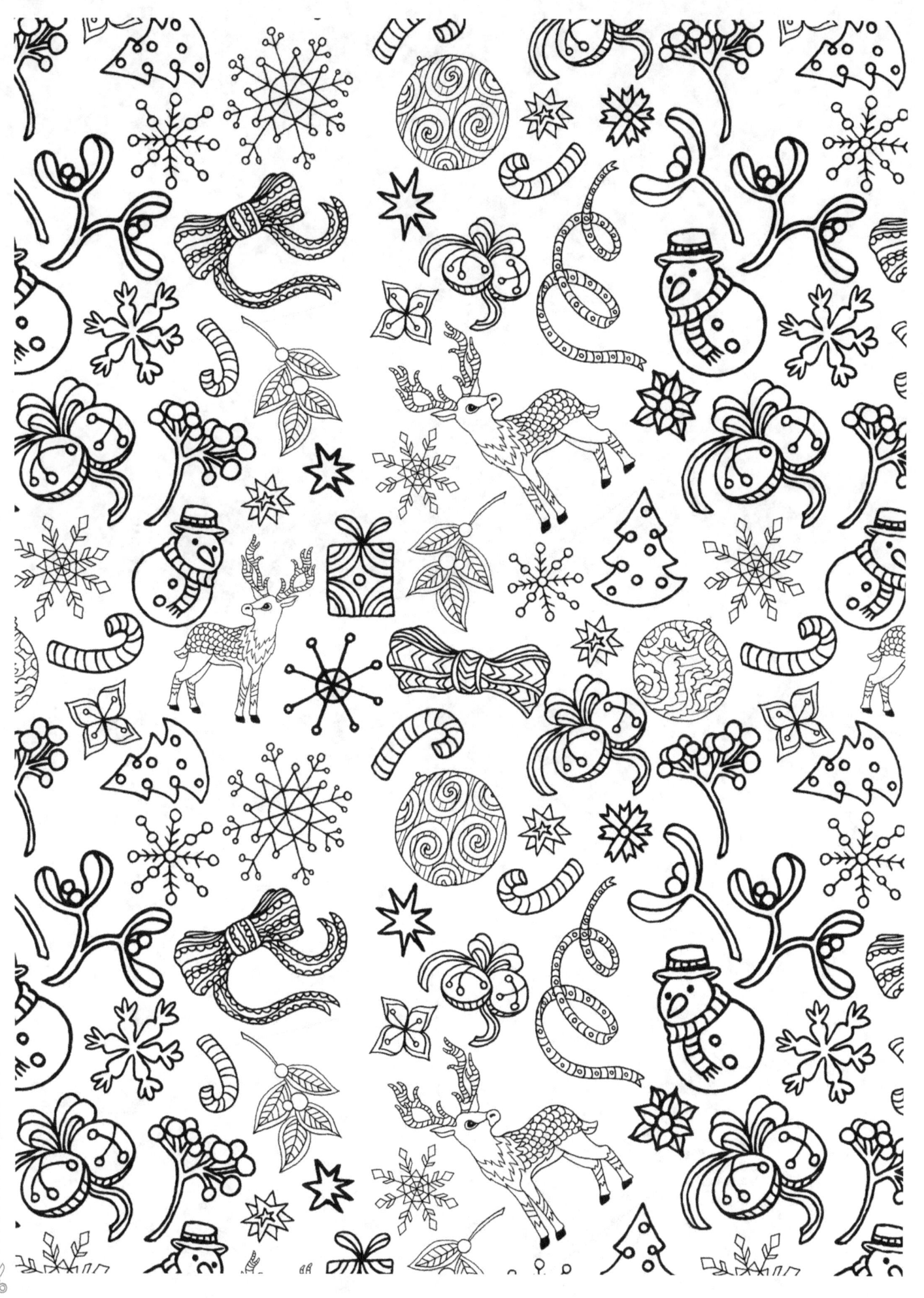

The merry family gatherings - the old, the very young; the strangely lovely way they harmonize in carols sung. For Christmas is tradition time -traditions that recall the precious memories down the years, the sameness of them all.

Helen Lowric Marshall

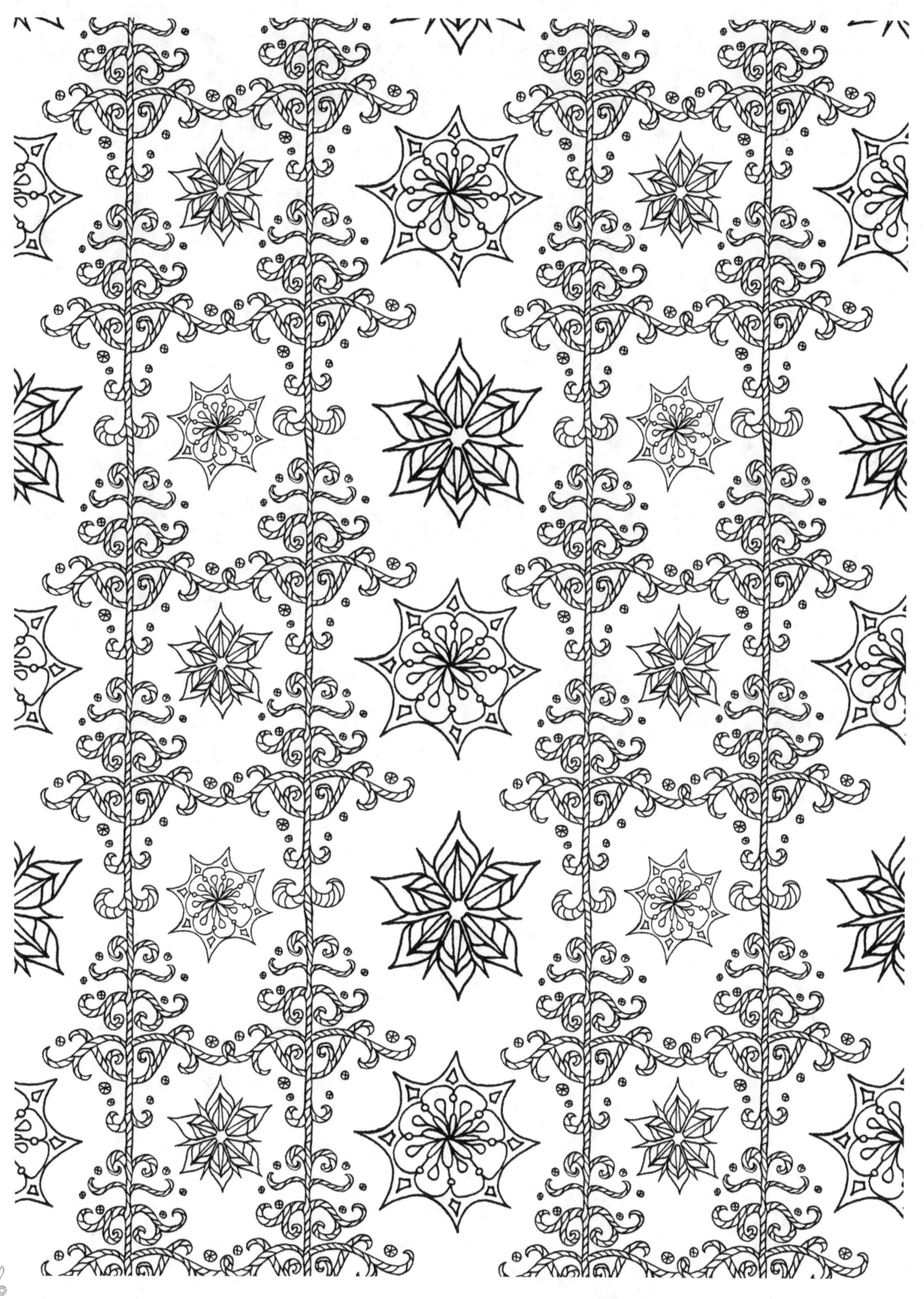

Christmas is forever, not for just one day, for loving, sharing, giving, are not to put away like bells and lights and tinsel, in some box upon a shelf. The good you do for others is good you do yourself.

Norman Wesley Brooks

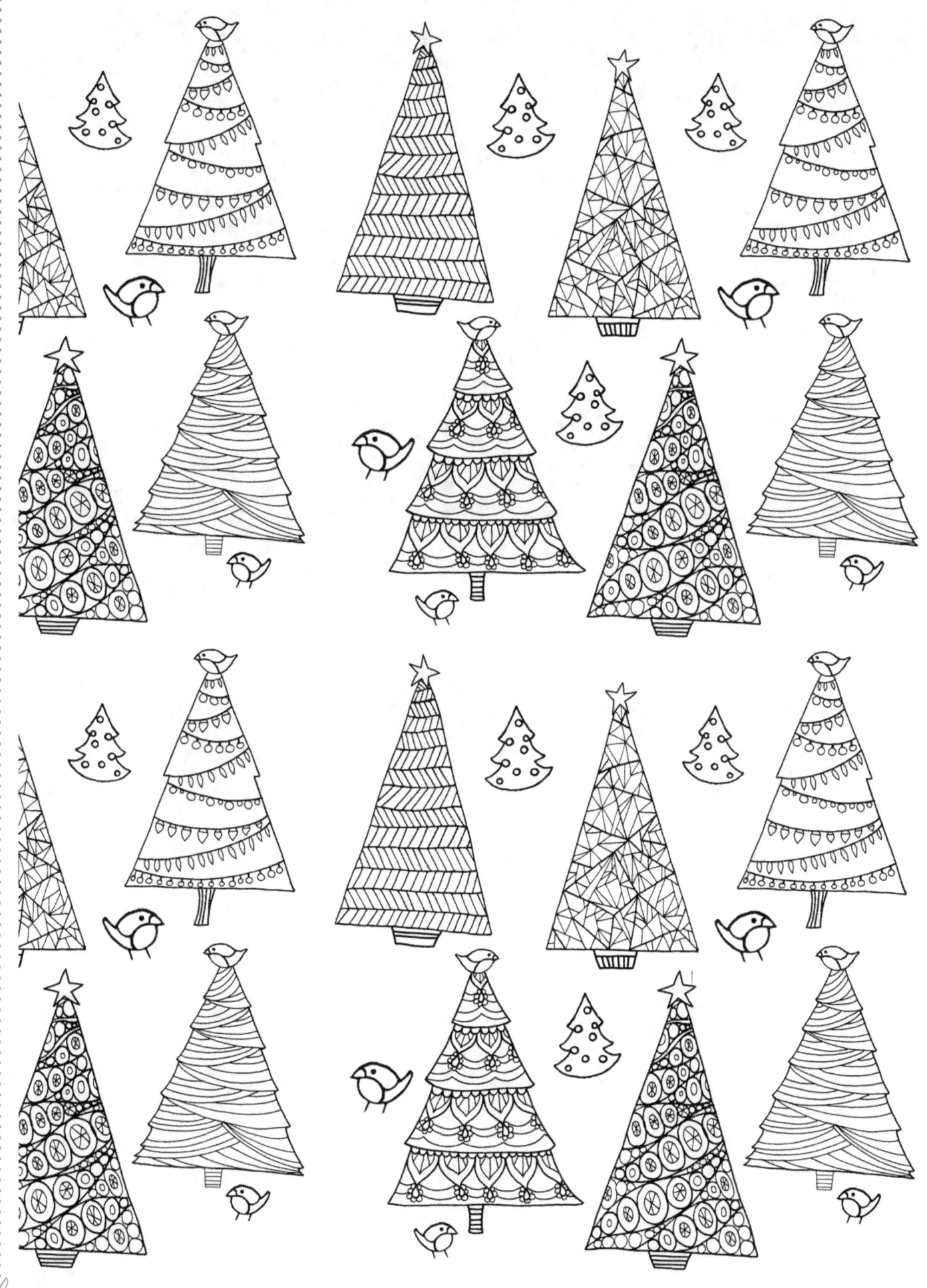

This time of year means being kind to everyone we meet, so share a smile with strangers we may pass along the street.

Betty Black

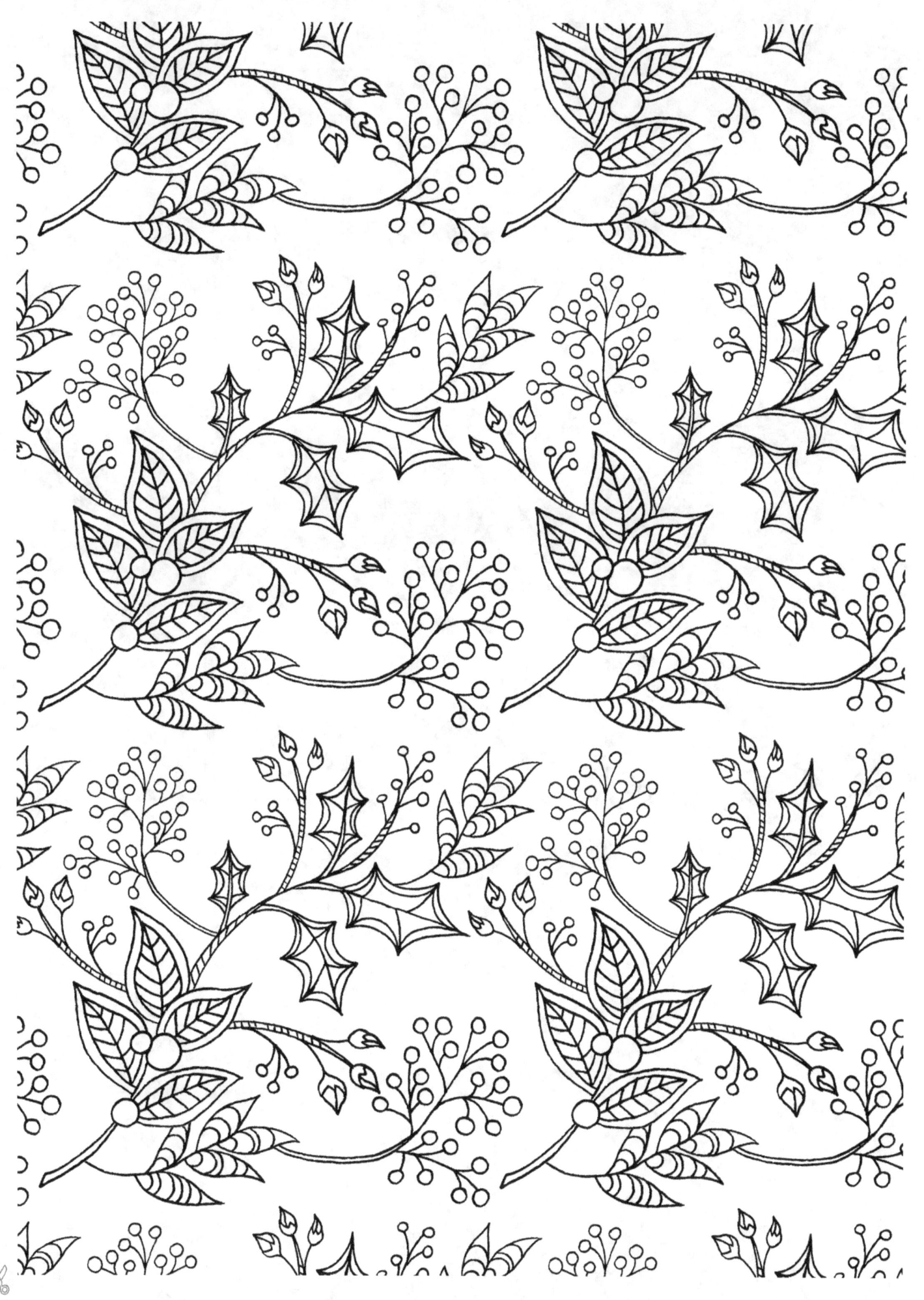

There is a Christmas song upon the air, There is a joy innate within the heart; An inner sense of peace, a holy light Illumines life and sets these days apart.

Edna Greene Hines

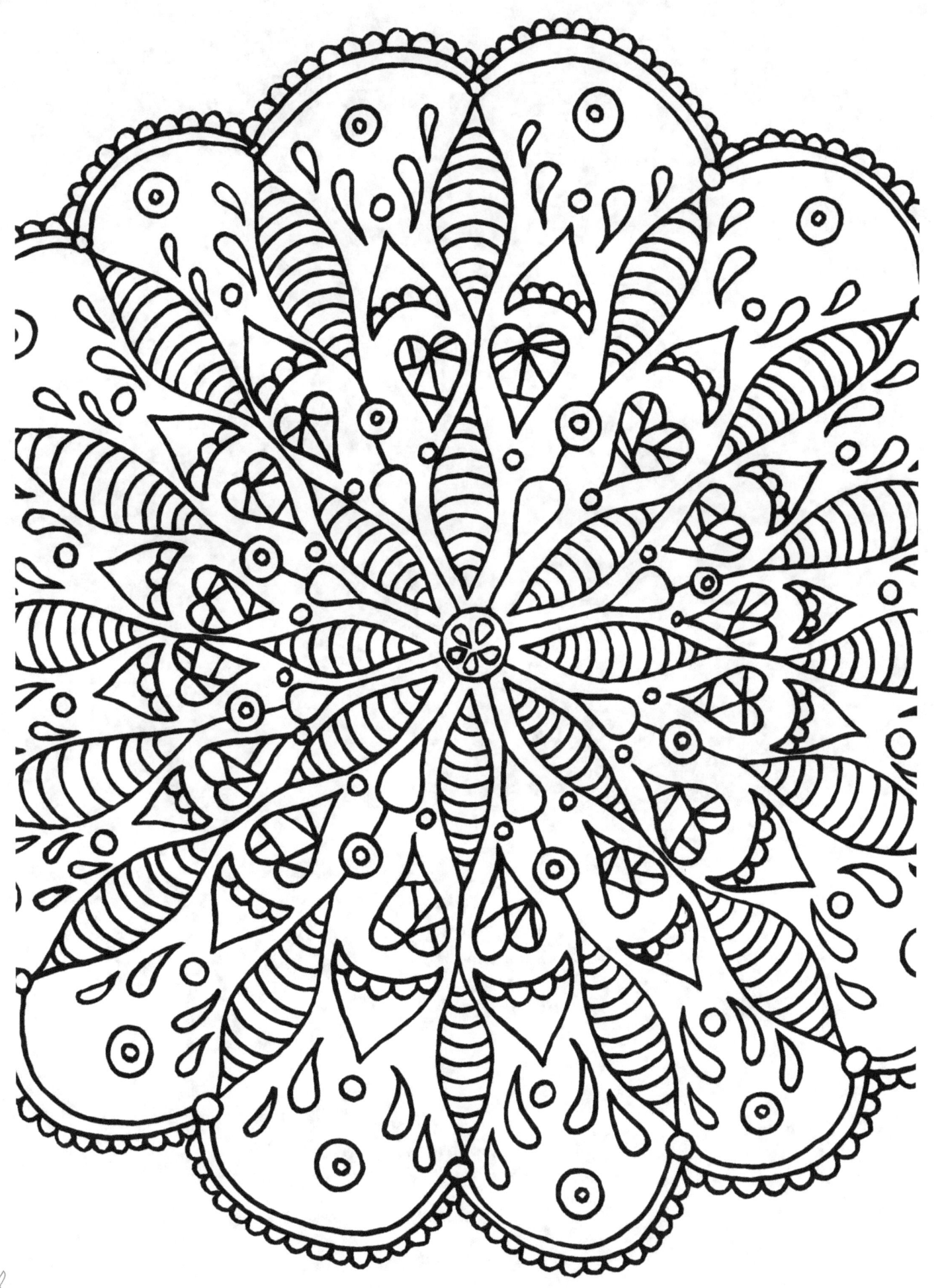

If I could wish a wish for you, it would be for peace and happiness not only now, but for the whole year through!

Catherine Pulsifer

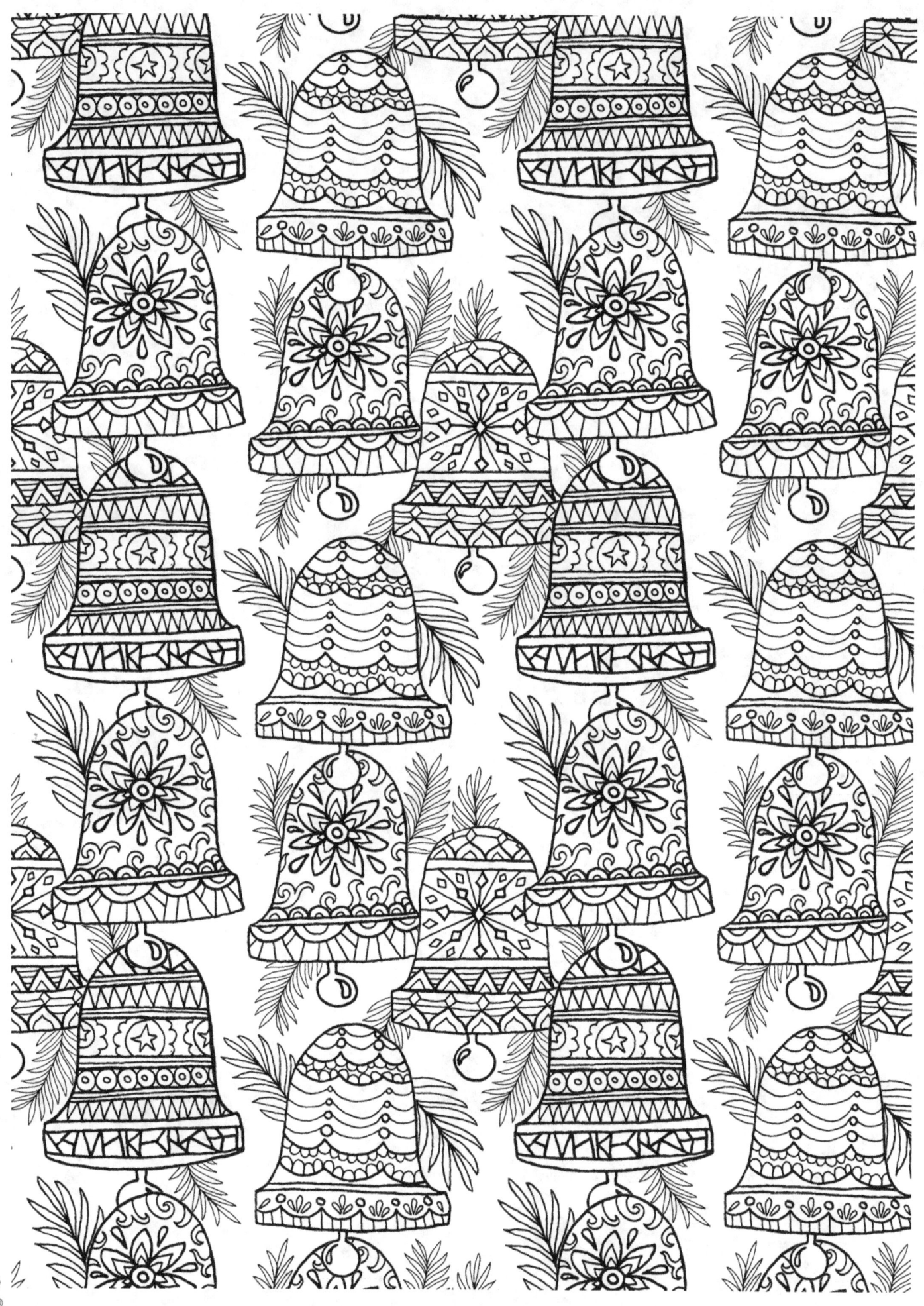

From home to home, and heart to heart, from one place to another. The warmth and joy of Christmas, brings us closer to each other.

Emily Matthews

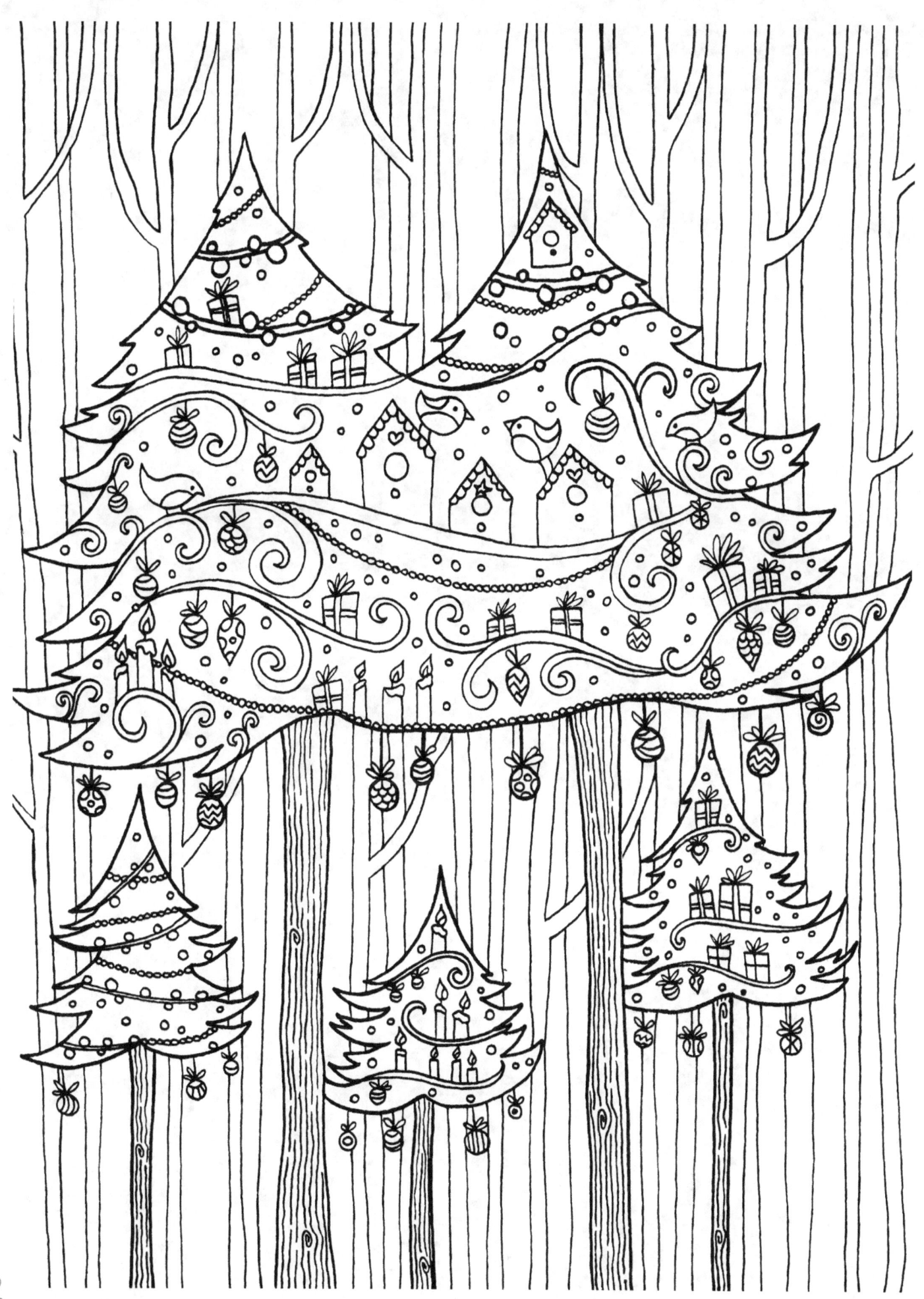

Also by Christina Rose

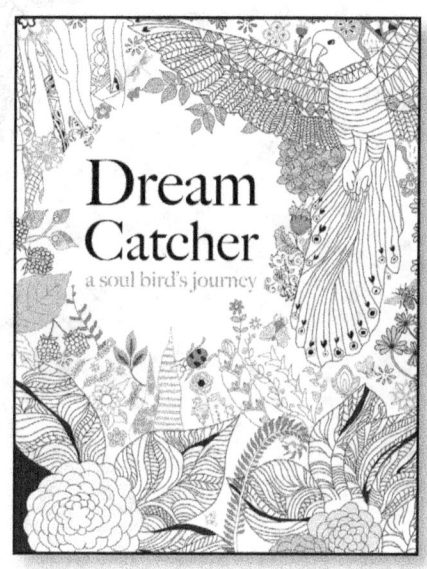

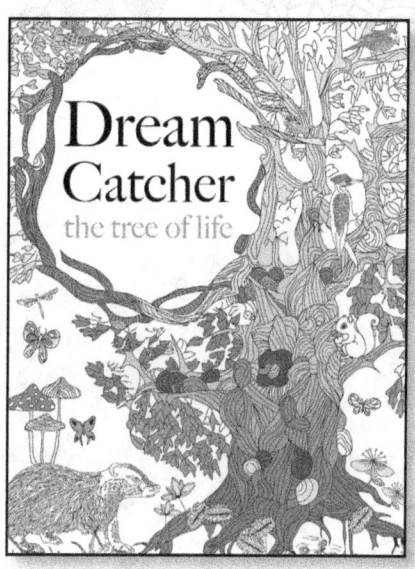

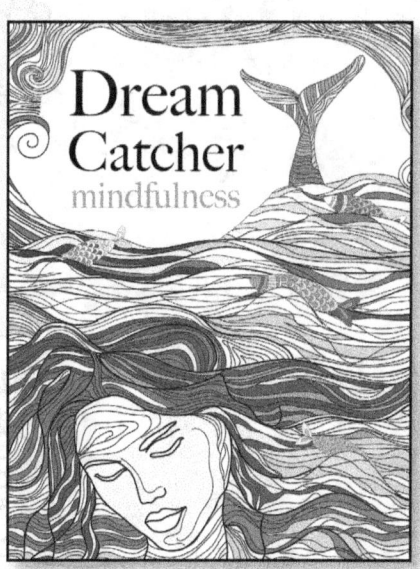

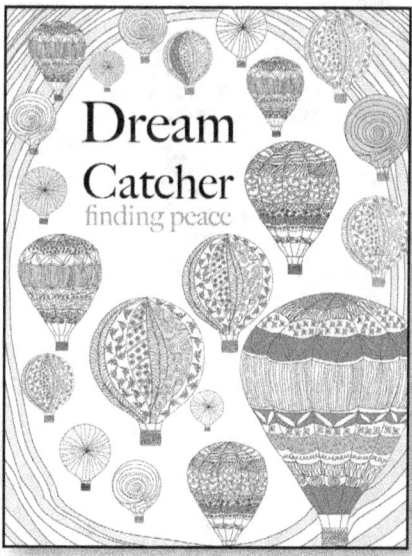

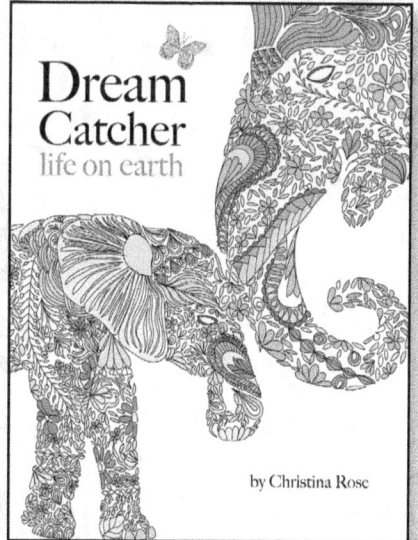